THE BATTLE
BELONGS TO THE
LORD

THE BATTLE
BELONGS TO THE
LORD

THE POWER OF SCRIPTURE FOR
DEFENDING OUR FAITH

K. SCOTT OLIPHINT

PUBLISHING
P.O. BOX 817 • PHILLIPSBURG • NEW JERSEY 08865-0817

Page design by Tobias Design
Typesetting by Lakeside Design Plus

Printed in the United States of America

Library of Congress Cataloging-in-Publication Data

Oliphint, K. Scott, 1955–
   The battle belongs to the Lord : the power of Scripture for defending our faith
  K. Scott Oliphint.
     p. cm.
  Includes bibliographical references and index.
  ISBN 0-87552-561-X (pbk.)
  1. Apologetics. I. Title.

BT1103.O45 2003
239—dc22

2003059624

To Jared, Joel, and Bonnie—apologists

CONTENTS

PREFACE

THIS BOOK IS MEANT to be an introduction—and a beginning—to a lifetime of defending and commending the Christian faith. Its goal is to point you to biblical principles that will provide a foundation for that task.

One way to work through this book is to use it in personal (or group) study. The questions at the end of each chapter, as their title notes, are meant to be used as *study* questions. Their answers will likely not be found directly in their respective chapters. The principles that can help with the answers, however, should be found in those chapters. The questions are provided in order to promote deeper thinking about defending and commending the faith. They are meant to be *discussion* questions; they will be most beneficial if discussed with others. In discussing them, try to think of actual, or at least possible, situations in which the principles studied could be applied.

INTRODUCTION

A STUDENT REPORTED to me recently that he had re-
turned from a conference entitled "Defending the Faith."
When I asked him what the most significant thing about it was,
I was surprised at his answer. He said the thing that most
caught his attention was one speaker's comments that went
something like this: "This year our topic is apologetics,[1] so you
really won't need to have your Bibles with you." The comment
was not meant to be humorous or flippant; it was simply a statement of fact.

A comment like this is understandable, though lamentable.
It is understandable, given the typical context and concerns of
apologetics these days. Typically, the context of apologetics has
been first of all philosophical. The vast majority of apologetic
discussions have taken place within philosophical walls, using
philosophical arguments, trying to reach philosophical conclusions. The language that has been used, the methods of argumentation, and the topics chosen for debate have been molded
primarily by a philosophical agenda.

In some ways, this is understandable, perhaps even natural.
There is, of course, an obvious overlap between apologetics and
philosophy. Because philosophy seeks to ask and answer the

1. We will be looking more closely at the word *apologetics* in the chapters that follow. For now, we can summarize its meaning simply as "a defense of the Christian faith."

1

"big" questions—What is the universe like? Who am I? How can I know anything? What is the nature of right and wrong?— its concerns are similar to some of the main concerns of the Christian faith. However, philosophy's answers to these questions have often been antagonistic to Christian truth. So, in response, Christian apologists have attempted to give Christian answers to philosophical questions—often using terms that philosophers would use and understand.

This is not a bad thing in and of itself. If Christianity can provide answers (and it can) to some of the most sophisticated and perplexing problems of life and thought, then we ought to be happy, and eager, to engage the debate. Problems arise, however, when the philosophical concerns *determine* the very nature of apologetics. The problem is that apologetics has become a largely philosophical discipline. So, it is not surprising that this student would attend a conference on Christian apologetics and never open the Bible. In philosophy one needs strong reasoning skills, not revelation (or so we're often told).

There is another reason for thinking that the Bible is not useful or needed in apologetics. It has to do with what is considered to be our *source* of truth. One of the ideas that has motivated apologists down through the centuries is that reason, not revelation, is the proper source of truth for apologetics. This is a controversial subject that cannot be settled here.

The basic approach of this position, however, has been to argue that there are areas of Christian truth—areas like the existence of God, the nature of the world, etc.—that are accessible to all of us, given the proper use of reason (proper assumptions and arguments). If these things are accessible to all of us, there is no immediate need to appeal to revelation for our discussion. We need only use our minds and appeal to universal principles—or to anything except revelation.

As a matter of fact, there is a strong and vocal tradition in apologetics that rejects any appeal to revelation when discussing apologetics. Such an appeal is thought to be illegitimate, in part, because the unbeliever does not accept biblical revelation at all. To appeal to biblical revelation as a part of our defense of the faith, then, would be to miss the concerns of the unbeliever altogether. What is needed, it is thought, is an appeal to what we all have in common. So, apologetics has been concerned, for the most part, to appeal to our "common" reason or our "common" principles of thought.

These trends have had a number of unfortunate effects. Most importantly, they have minimized the use of Scripture in apologetics. Of course, if reason is all we need to properly defend the faith, then the Bible need not concern us in that task (unlike, say, evangelism or preaching). But is reason all that we really need to defend the Christian faith?

The net effect of this notion, that reason is the proper context for apologetics, is that apologetics becomes more of a hobby for intellectuals than something of life-and-death significance. As a result, the discipline of apologetics is often seen to belong somewhere between art history and the Christian Doctors Association—interesting for some, but not relevant to most Christians. This view of apologetics extends even to institutions that train students for gospel ministry. Since apologetics is thought to be only marginally helpful to Christians, virtually every theological seminary that I know of places its courses in apologetics on the list of electives—unnecessary for ministry, but perhaps interesting to those who are so inclined.

But we should all be "so inclined." The purpose of this book is to get us to open our Bibles again when we think about apologetics. Of course, if apologetics *is* a kind of "side dish" along-side the main course of Christian truth, then it might be proper not to depend on Scripture for any direct information. So one of the things that we will claim in chapter 1 is that apologetics is essential to our Christian lives; it is, in fact, required of every Christian.

That may sound overwhelming to some who have just been introduced to this subject. But there is no need to be intimidated. We will see that apologetics is, in its most basic form, simply the application of biblical truth to the concerns of the day. As an application of biblical truth, all Christians have what they need to do apologetics. If the Lord commands us to defend the faith once for all given to the saints, then he has given us what we need to fulfill that command.

In one sense, the entire Bible is an apologetic. It is given as God's word. It comes to us as truth to tell us who God is and what he requires of us. Most of it comes into a "hostile" environment, an environment flooded with the effects of sin and rebellion. But because it comes as truth to a hostile world, it challenges the worldviews and opinions of those who would want to oppose its truth.

When the Bible begins with "In the beginning, God . . . ," it is immediately giving us the most foundational of truths, but it is also confronting any view that seeks to deny this God. The history of redemption is also a history of revelation. God reveals himself to Adam in the garden. After the Fall, God's revelation comes into the world through the prophets "at many times and in many ways" (Hebrews 1:1). It comes to challenge unbelief and to reveal the Lord's will to those who trust him.

It comes, preeminently, in these last days, in his Son. Jesus
Christ comes into the world *as the truth itself,* in order to preach
repentance, since, with his coming, the kingdom of heaven is
near (Matthew 3:2).

The idea of repentance has a distinctly intellectual side to
it. Of course, that does not make it coldly intellectualistic; repentance has much more to it than simply a change of mind.
But its focus is on the mind. Repentance means, at least, that
our mind-set must change with respect to a certain lifestyle or
way of thinking. Repentance, as we will see, must be a part of
our apologetic appeal. We dare not simply think that our responsibility in apologetics is to show that *some* deity might exist
somewhere. Our responsibility is to tell the truth, the truth about
Christianity, including the truth that God now "commands all
people everywhere to repent" (Acts 17:30). We seek and desire,
in defending the faith, to see a change of mind in those to whom
we speak.

If I were to summarize the next few chapters in a paragraph
that would capture our responsibility to defend the faith, it
would look something like this:

> Since Christ is Lord, and the battle is his, we must al-
> ways be ready to contend for the faith once for all de-
> livered to the saints. We must use the weapons, not of
> this world, but of the Lord. We must take every thought
> captive to the obedience of Christ as we demolish the
> arguments, with gentleness and reverence, of those who
> suppress the truth in unrighteousness, exchanging the
> truth of God for a lie, worshiping created things, rather
> than the Creator, who is blessed forever. Amen.

As you read through this book, this statement will, I hope, take on new and clearer meaning for you.

As one who teaches apologetics in a seminary (where it is required for ministerial training), I am more convinced now than when I first began learning the subject as a new Christian that its emphasis is needed in our churches today. It is needed, not simply to give us "ammunition" against the enemy, though that is one of its purposes, but also to give us a biblical perspective on "every wind of doctrine" that blows our way in the stormy seas of our world. With the proper biblical preparation, we can be confident, not only that we, by God's grace, have answers to give to those who ask, but that "the whole counsel of God" (Acts 20:27) is the only true and helpful response to those questions.

THE LORD'S BATTLE

Saul was convinced that David was too small and too young to go to battle, especially against a giant! He looked at the evidence, sized up the situation, and came to what appeared to be a logical conclusion. A young boy, he thought, is not capable of defeating a giant:

> And Saul said to David, "You are not able to go against this Philistine to fight with him, for you are but a youth, and he has been a man of war from his youth." (1 Samuel 17:33)

Almost anyone assessing the situation would have easily come to Saul's conclusion. But he had missed a very important point. Sometimes the plans and purposes of God defy the obvious. David, unlike Saul, knew that this was just such a time.

It was true that David was inexperienced. He had never fought in a war, while Goliath was an accomplished warrior. But David remembered something that Saul had forgotten. He remembered that "the battle is the LORD's" (1 Samuel 17:47), and that made all the difference.

If we think of apologetics as a spiritual continuation of David's battle with Goliath, it may help us to see some important and encouraging truths as we seek to defend and commend the Christian faith. The first truth is simple, and it bears repeating time and time again: *The battle is the Lord's*. There will come a time when the battle will be no more. The end of history will mark the end of the spiritual battle on earth. Until that time, however, the Lord will continue to use the likes of us in the war against the forces of darkness in the heavenly places.

This is a great privilege. But it can become terrifying, and we can easily despair of all hope if, like Saul, we forget just whose battle we are fighting. Because it is the Lord's battle, to depend on our own strength or expertise would be folly. He is the Lord Sabaoth—the Lord of hosts—and he continues to command his army. His purpose in this command is to bring glory *to* himself by saving a people *for* himself. Since the battle is the Lord's, it is to be waged in his way.

We must also remember that the Lord is the primary and all-powerful participant in this battle. He is the commander of his own army (Joshua 5:14). As such, he leads his people into battle, stays to fight along with them, and, in the end, assures victory.

What was behind Saul's forgetfulness? Why did he forget whose battle he was in? The answer is that he allowed what was visible to overshadow what was invisible. He had taken on a worldly perspective. So he was defeated even before he began.

But David saw the invisible. He knew whose battle it was, and he knew his place in that battle.

There are three principles that David applied in his battle with Goliath that we should remember as we begin to think about apologetics. They have to do with the reason for the battle, its purpose, and its weapons. Some of these things will be discussed in the chapters that follow, but they should help us set our focus here.

(1) The *reason* David went out to face the giant was simple:

> Then David said to the Philistine, "You come to me with a sword and with a spear and with a javelin, but I come to you in the name of the LORD of hosts, the God of the armies of Israel, whom you have defied." (1 Samuel 17:45)

David knew that the battle was not about him. He was not concerned to defend his own honor or his own reputation. As a matter of fact, David seems to have given no thought to himself at all. The reason he faced Goliath was that *Goliath had defied the Lord of hosts*. Goliath had issued a challenge to Israel. In that challenge, he was defying the armies of Israel (v. 10) and asserting himself and his power. He thought that he was greater and stronger than the armies of God. He continued his proud abuse for forty days (v. 16).

Saul and Israel were afraid of Goliath. But David saw Goliath's challenge for what it was. It was not a challenge simply to Israel. It was more than that. In defying Israel's armies, Goliath was defying the Commander of the armies as well. Goliath's challenge was a challenge to the glory and power and honor of the Lord of hosts.

David was concerned for the glory of the Lord. He was not concerned to show that Israel was, in itself, stronger than the

Philistines. He was not concerned to display more strength than Goliath. He knew that Goliath's challenge went far beyond the Valley of Elah. It was a cosmic challenge. It was a challenge to the truth of Israel's God. It was primarily a challenge to the Truth himself.

When we seek to respond to challenges that come to us, challenges to the truth of Christianity, we should always remember that it is God's glory—his power and goodness and holiness and truth—that we are defending. Of course, God is perfectly capable of defending himself. Surely the only one who is all-powerful can better defend his honor than others whose power and goodness are severely limited. So why should we try to defend the glory and truth of God?

That is the mystery and the beauty of it all. The Lord of hosts has seen fit, in his own secret wisdom and providence, to use the likes of us to fight the cosmic battle. We have to admit that, from our own limited and sinful vantage point, this looks like trying to drain an ocean with a straw. But God's ways are perfect (Deuteronomy 32:4); whatever he does is right and true (Isaiah 45:19). His determination to use us in the cosmic fight fits perfectly with his perfect plan. It becomes, then, our privilege and honor to serve him in this way.

That is why David was quick to volunteer for the fight. It may just be that *because* David was the youngest, he was ready for battle. Being the youngest in a family in Israel normally meant being, in many ways, the least significant. Surely David had understood from an early age that his position in the family gave him the fewest family privileges. He was, in many ways, the weakest of all, and he was well aware of his weaknesses. In realizing his weaknesses, however, David could not have imagined that he had the power to fight with the armies of Israel. If he was going to fight, it would have to be the Lord who would do battle through him.

So it is with us. If we ever think that we are capable, in and of ourselves, to fight the Lord's battle, we lose the battle altogether. The Lord uses the weak in the world to shame the strong; he uses the simple to confound the strong and mighty. He does that, as Paul reminds us, so that no one will have occasion to boast (1 Corinthians 1:27–29).

David was willing to fight because his Lord had been challenged. Goliath's persistence in defying Israel's God was an act of cosmic rebellion. This was not about land or turf or a human kingdom. This was about God's rightful rule over his creation. Goliath had challenged that rule. David could not let the challenge go unanswered.

(2) David announced his *purpose* in this battle. He actually announced three related purposes. First, David answered Goliath's challenge, so "that all the earth may know that there is a God in Israel" (1 Samuel 17:46). How did David's response accomplish that purpose?

The answer to that question would have been obvious to anyone standing there that day. The only way that David could hope to defeat this giant warrior was if Someone more powerful was fighting with him. The odds against David were so great that only some kind of powerful intervention could save him. The natural conclusion to this confrontation was clear. It would take someone *supernatural* to overcome the natural. If David actually defeated Goliath, it would then be clear that there was a God in Israel.

In this battle, David was concerned to declare the knowledge of God throughout the world. As we will see, knowing God is a central and essential part of our defense. It has always been a goal of apologetics that people come to acknowledge him.

Discussions about God—what he has done, why we should believe in him, etc.—have been central in the history of apologetics at least since the early Middle Ages.

David's concern in this battle was to demonstrate that the God of Israel was the true God. Goliath had his gods, but he could not rely on them to fight his battles. Goliath was dependent on his own (almost superhuman) strength and power. David's God, the true God of Israel, would not have his people depend on themselves. If the battle was to be fought as the Lord's battle, then *his* strength and power had to be central. Any victory would reveal something of who this God was.

Second, David announced that he was fighting "that all this assembly may know that the Lord saves" (1 Samuel 17:47). The remarkable thing about this announcement was just how insignificant David saw himself to be in this battle. While being confident of victory, he was just as sure that it was the Lord who would achieve that victory. The Lord, and he alone, saves his people.

This does not mean, of course, that the Lord would have conquered Goliath if David had not gone out against him. The Lord could have won without David, but he chose instead to give David the privilege of being an instrument in the victory.

So it is with our apologetic battles. The Lord could save people, he could draw each and every one to himself, without any effort from us. But he has decided not to work that way (see Romans 10). The important point, however, is that we should see ourselves as David saw himself in this battle. Whatever salvation may come through our efforts, *it is the Lord who saves*. Notice, David did not say that he and the Lord would save Israel. He did not view this as a cooperative effort. David knew who alone has the power to save, and he gave credit where credit was due. He gave glory where it belonged. All glory goes to God alone in salvation.

Third, David did not simply acknowledge that the Lord saves. Rather, he declared *how* he saves as well: "that all this assembly may know that the LORD saves not with sword and spear" (1 Samuel 17:47). Why was it important for David that the Lord does not save with sword or spear? Was he simply implying that the Lord uses slingshots instead of spears? Is the point that the Lord's weapons are smaller?

(3) This brings us to the principle regarding David's *weapons* in his battle with Goliath: The Lord does not use the weapons of battle at all to save his people. The Lord's battle is a battle for people. It is not a war over turf. He is not concerned simply to give his people more land. He is concerned to own *them,* to redeem them, to buy them back. With that concern, swords and spears are ineffective. What is needed in the Lord's battle are weapons that will cause people to bow down, to bend the knee and acknowledge that the Lord, and he alone, is God. Only supernatural weapons can accomplish that task.

This does not mean, as we saw above, that the Lord uses *no* means, or weapons, to accomplish his purposes. Although he could have stopped Goliath's heart without David, he chose to use David and his sling. He chose the weak and simple things so that those who relied on what they thought to be powerful and mighty things would be put to shame.

We may be called on by God to battle experienced warriors as we defend and commend the faith. We may be brought into situations where we are weak and frail, though our opponent is strong and mighty (at least by the world's standards). That seems to be exactly the kind of situation in which the Lord likes to show forth his power and glory.

Of course, if it is the Lord's battle, there will never be a time when we will meet someone who is more powerful or more able. Because the Lord is the commander, anyone with whom we speak will be weak and frail by comparison.

We need David's perspective as we think about defending the faith. We must have David's *faith* if we are going to do battle at all. We will not use the weapons of the world. We will fight, if we fight the Lord's battle, with his weapons. And the chief weapon that he has given to us is his sword, the Word of God itself.

We must disagree with that conference speaker. The Bible should be central to any discussion of apologetics. It is the Bible that we need, and must open, if we are going to think about apologetics and begin to prepare to do it. To fight the Lord's battle without the Lord's sword is foolishness. To fail to use the only weapon that is able to pierce to the heart, is to fight a losing battle. The following chapters are meant to help us see what "God's sword," his Word, says about fighting his battles. Without that Word, our fight will be in vain. With it, however, we may be assured of pleasing him (and therefore of achieving "success") as we fight.

> Fierce may be the conflict, strong may be the foe,
> But the King's own army none can overthrow:
> Round his standard ranging, vict'ry is secure;
> For his truth unchanging makes the triumph sure.
> Joyfully enlisting by thy grace divine,
> We are on the Lord's side, Savior, we are thine.
> (Frances R. Havergal)

"For the battle is the LORD's, and he will give you into our hand" (1 Samuel 17:47).

YOUR MASTER PROCLAIM

"IT SEEMS TO ME," said Marv, "that the best account of human behavior is the one given to us by Sigmund Freud. Freud was brilliant. He was a master of observation. He spent years of his life attempting to find out what makes us 'tick.' I can't understand how we could disagree with him. His theories have been proven time and time again. How can you believe in Christianity, given what Freud has told us?"

This statement, in substance, was made recently in my own home, by a friend of my teenage son. How would you respond to Marv? How would you begin to respond to his allegiance to Freud? How would you explain your own allegiance to Christ? What if you had never read anything written by Freud?

Challenges to our faith can come from any quarter. They may come from friends at school or at work, or from strangers on an airplane or at the store. They can come at various times and in various ways. They may come directly or indirectly. Someone may simply say, in passing, that the only thing worth

> *But in your hearts regard Christ the Lord as holy, always being prepared to make a defense to anyone who asks you for a reason for the hope that is in you; yet do it with gentleness and respect, having a good conscience, so that, when you are slandered, those who revile your good behavior in Christ may be put to shame. For it is better to suffer for doing good, if that should be God's will, than for doing evil. —1 Peter 3:15–17*

believing in is yourself, or someone may try to convince you that belief in Christ is a mindless exercise. How do we respond to such things? Should we try to avoid them?

Every Christian is called by God to give an answer to such challenges. Giving an answer when challenges come is what we mean by the word *apologetics*. Apologetics does *not* mean saying you're sorry. Quite the opposite, it means defending and commending, not excusing, the faith.

All of us are asked to be ready to give a reason for our belief and our trust in Christ. If God requires us to give an answer, then surely he has provided the resources we need. The Lord has both commanded the Christian to carry out the task of apologetics and equipped the Christian to do so. This may not sound like good news, particularly since the word *apologetics* is confusing and often misunderstood. It is likely, however, that many of us have been doing apologetics without even knowing it.

Those who have been Christians for a while may already know what it is like to defend the truth of Christianity when questions and objections arise. This is as it should be. The Lord wants us to respond to such challenges. If we look closely at 1 Peter 3:15, we should be better able to determine what the task of defending the Christian faith is, and what our responsibility is as we carry out that task.

Hard Times

Times were difficult for the first Christians after the resurrection of their Lord and Savior. There was much opposition to the Christian faith, both from within the church and from the political and religious forces outside the church. This opposition, Paul reminds us, was part of a perpetual heavenly battle that rages wherever the forces of darkness try to subvert the truth of Christ and destroy his church (Ephesians 6:12).

As Peter writes his first epistle, Christians are experiencing persecution. They are being persecuted simply because they are Christians. Is that why Peter says they are scattered (1 Peter 1:1)? Commentators differ, but Peter's clear intent is to emphasize that being a Christian at this time will bring persecution with it. These Christians are a dispersed group, a suffering group, and they are experiencing, as Peter writes to them, the unjust punishment of the civil government.

How should a Christian act in these circumstances? How should we respond when it appears that the world around us is opposed to the truth? Are we to hide until things improve? Wait for a more sympathetic government? Long for days gone by? Before looking specifically at 1 Peter 3, we should notice how Peter begins this epistle. He answers those questions with at least two hints in the first chapter.

Who We Are

"Peter, an apostle of Jesus Christ, To those who are elect exiles . . ." (1 Peter 1:1). One of the fascinating things about genealogy is the sense of connectedness that can come from knowing the family tree. The more we know about our family, the more rooted we feel. We can often follow the family's movement from another country and imagine the difficulties they must have faced. It is often an encouragement to know something about our family roots.

Likewise, the first thing that we must remember when facing challenges to our faith is our spiritual roots; we must remember where we have come from. We are, as Peter says, the elect of God (1 Peter 1:1). Our identity lies in the fact that God has set his eternal love on us. He has chosen us. Our true identity is in him alone. If someone were to ask us one of the most perplexing of questions—Who are you?—what would our initial response be? Most of us would first give our name, and then perhaps say what we do, followed by family information.

As natural as that response would be, we should not lose sight of the fact that those answers do not define who we *really* are. They do indicate important information about us. But when all the outer layers are stripped away, our most basic identity is defined by our relationship to our Creator. Christians are, at bottom, children of God. Our identity is wrapped up in the identity of the one who gave us new birth. We are children of God, first and foremost.

This is Peter's counsel to his readers. Of course, he has his Jewish readers in mind first of all. The Lord's people in the Old Testament knew about persecution. They had been taken into captivity. They also knew that their deliverance from suffering would come by God's grace alone (Deuteronomy 7:6ff.). But Peter also has his Gentile readers in mind. They know that Jesus Christ has broken down the ethnic barrier. They now know that all who believe are children of God (Galatians 3:7; Ephesians 2:14). Their identity rests in the first place in what God has done for and in them, not in what their circumstances are.

No matter what happens to them, they are and always will be, by God's grace, his children.

Because we are identified, first and foremost, as God's children, we are "exiles," or strangers, in this world. The Greek word that Peter uses for "exiles" is a word that emphasizes the temporary character of the place in which we find ourselves. It refers to the passing character of this world. This would have been understood immediately by Peter's audience. They had just recently been scattered across parts of Asia Minor. They knew that where they were living was not their home. Those who are chosen by God become citizens of *his* kingdom.

This citizenship makes any other place of residence both temporary and foreign. Anyone who has spent some time in a foreign country knows how uncomfortable and odd things can be, compared to "home." I recently spent some time in a foreign country. All sense of time was different; the sun came up and went down at different times. The money was different. Measurements were different. Whether I was on the road or in the kitchen, in a car or on the street, outside or inside the house, nearly everything that was a part of my daily routine was different. I was a stranger in that world.

That is how Christians are in this world. As citizens of another place, we are not "at home" here on planet Earth. At least, we shouldn't be. Peter is concerned to remind his readers of that truth as they live in a culture that is foreign to them, both physically and spiritually.

It is easy for us—it may even be natural for us—to think of this world as the focus of our lives. We pour so much time and energy into the things that surround us. That in itself is not bad. We are commanded by God to work heartily here in this life (Colossians 3:23). In some ways, we are supposed to "pour ourselves into" what we do here. We are placed in circumstances by God's providence and are to make the most of them (Ephesians 5:16). We are called by God to do our work for his glory (1 Corinthians 10:31). All of this takes an enormous amount of time and energy. It almost unconsciously causes us to be intent about the things that are around us. We devote ourselves to what we do because the Lord wants us to do all things as if we were doing them for him.

The point that Peter is concerned to make, however, is that our status as strangers should always qualify and modify our good and needful activities in this world. Our "strangeness" should set the perspective for us as we seek to live in this world for the glory of our Savior. While we should do our work heartily here in this world, we should never let the things of this world possess us. We should think of ourselves as only temporarily residing where we are. We do our work, and live in this place, while we wait for our true home.

Given that Christians are strangers, the contrast that Peter presents in the first two verses of chapter 1 is striking. While it is true that these Christians are scattered throughout "Pontus, Galatia, Cappadocia, Asia, and Bithynia," they are also God's elect, who have been chosen "according to the foreknowledge of God the Father, in the sanctification of the Spirit, for obedience to Jesus Christ and for sprinkling with his blood." The emphasis here is not on the "scatteredness" of the Lord's people, but rather on their "rootedness" in God's choice, based squarely on his eternal love, and effected through his Son's blood and his Spirit's sanctifying work.

We all need this kind of reminder. It is especially needed by those who are in the midst of persecution. Peter tells his readers that this world is not their home; they are only passing through. Their home is with him who is working out all things for their good, by his Son's blood, through his Spirit (1:2).

WHO HE IS

> Though you have not seen him, you love him. Though you do not now see him, you believe in him and rejoice with joy that is inexpressible and filled with glory, obtaining the outcome of your faith, the salvation of your souls. (1:8–9)

The fact that God is invisible can greatly increase our perplexity. It may seem especially perplexing when we are in pain or afraid. Those are times when we want someone to be with us. We may think that if we could only see God, even for a moment, then we could persevere when trials come.

We often speak of "seeing a light at the end of the tunnel." We need some encouragement when things grow dark; we need to know—*to see*—the light. It is much easier to endure the darkness if the light is visible to us. But the true Light is not visible; he is essentially invisible (1 Timothy 1:17). Even though we affirm that biblical truth, we still long, at times, to see God.

This longing is a good thing, though it can often serve to confuse us. We are people "of the senses." We are guided by our senses each day. And, for the most part, they are trustworthy guides. Nearly everything we do normally requires that we use and trust our senses. However, since we are always related to the world around us with our senses, it is all too easy to begin thinking that this world that we experience is all that there is. We might even begin to think, "If we cannot in some way 'sense' something, it is probably not real."

This was part of the problem with Thomas (John 20:26ff.). He had decided that he would believe that the crucified Christ had been raised only if he could see the evidence. And when he saw it, he was perfectly willing to submit and believe. It was in the seeing that Thomas believed.

We rightly note that this incident shows a weakness in Thomas. He illustrates what we should strive to avoid in the Christian life. But while it is easy for us in hindsight to criticize Thomas for his small faith, all of us have the same tendency. We, too, would rather see than trust. After all, for much of what we do in this world, seeing *is* believing.

This may explain why many Christians, even today, would rather see than believe. There are renewed efforts today to "show" that God is working by new "signs and wonders." Efforts are being made to locate God's acts of healing, so that he might become more "visible" to us. We want to see God's works in order to be assured that he is still with us.

But Peter does not encourage these suffering, scattered Christians to look for signs and wonders for their comfort. Instead, he reminds them, and us all, what the proper response to the invisible God should be. We will never see God. He would not be God if we could see him. Nevertheless, we are to love him and to believe in him.

Peter is simply reminding us of the apostle Paul's admonition—that the journey of the Christian, the "walk" of the Christian life on this side of heaven, is by faith and not by sight (2 Corinthians 5:7). That walk is by faith, at least in part, because God is invisible. There will never be a time when he is visible to us. We should learn to live properly now with the God who is invisible, so that we may live perfectly in eternity with the same invisible God.

Since God is and always will be invisible, and since it is our duty to love the Lord our God with all of our heart, soul, mind, and strength, our priority must be, in all circumstances, to set our minds on the invisible first of all. Paul, while experiencing persecution himself, reminds the Corinthian saints that it is the invisible things that are eternal (2 Corinthians 4:18). It is the invisible things that should shape our view of the visible, and not the other way around.

Peter's charge to these persecuted Christians is to set their minds on the invisible. He reminds them that they have already set their hearts there. Even though they do not see him, they love him. Now they must focus their efforts and attention on the God whom they love. They must remember their relationship to this invisible God, and remember that the one who is himself invisible is alone God. This is an important reminder for suffering Christians to hear.

This is just another part of what it means to be an "exile," an "alien" or a "stranger," in this world. The world around us is not our home. We train ourselves to focus on the unseen. So also the one who truly reigns is not the one we see in power, but the invisible one whom we see only by faith (see Hebrews 11).

It is in this context that we look at the central passage on apologetics in the New Testament, 1 Peter 3:15–16.

A PROPER FEAR

Persecution should cause us to remember at least two things. It should cause us to remember that this world is not our home, and it should cause us to remember to set our minds on things above, where Christ is (Colossians 3:1–2). Those two things have been Peter's focus as he writes to persecuted Christians.

Peter writes to tell these Christians how they should respond to those who would object to their beliefs or who would attack them for being Christians. The focus of his admonition begins in chapter 3, verse 8:

> Finally, all of you, have unity of mind, sympathy, brotherly love, a tender heart, and a humble mind.

It should not escape our notice that 1 Peter 3:1–7 focuses on family relationships. Peter knows that God has regulated the family in a certain way and that, at its root, the Christian community can never be sanctified if the families in it are not. He writes:

> Likewise, wives, be subject to your own husbands, so that even if some do not obey the word, they may be won without a word by the conduct of their wives— when they see your respectful and pure conduct. Do not let your adorning be external—the braiding of hair, the wearing of gold, or the putting on of clothing—but let your adorning be the hidden person of the heart with the imperishable beauty of a gentle and quiet spirit, which in God's sight is very precious. For this is how the holy women who hoped in God used to adorn themselves, by submitting to their husbands, as Sarah obeyed Abraham, calling him lord. And you are her children, if you do good and do not fear anything that is frightening. Likewise, husbands, live with your wives in an understanding way, showing honor to the woman as the weaker vessel, since they are heirs with you of the grace of life, so that your prayers may not be hindered. (1 Peter 3:1–7)

This point needs particular stress in our day. It is important for churches to think about reaching the lost, building up and edifying the saints, and making a difference in their communities. But we should never focus so much on the church's responsibilities that we miss what is even more important—the family. This aspect of Christian influence has suffered terribly in the last fifty years or so. And it should be said that the influence of the gospel will inevitably suffer with the breakdown of the Christian family. Peter reminds his readers of their roles in the family, so that their gospel witness might flourish.

How *should* Christians act in the face of opposition, opposition that may bring them harm? Peter remembers what he heard Jesus say in the Sermon on the Mount: "Do not repay evil for evil or reviling for reviling, but on the contrary, bless, for to this you were called, that you may obtain a blessing" (v. 9; cf. Matthew 5:11). Since Israel faced a similar situation in the Old Testament, Peter refers us in 3:14 to Isaiah 8, which was written to the Lord's people at a time when they were threatened by an invasion from the Assyrians:

> Do not call conspiracy all that this people calls conspiracy, and do not fear what they fear, nor be in dread. But the LORD of hosts, him you shall regard as holy. Let him be your fear, and let him be your dread. (Isaiah 8:12–13)

The Lord's command here goes right to the heart of the situation. In thinking of and quoting this passage from Isaiah, Peter takes up the subject of fear. In this case, the notion of fear is a broad one that can include a variety of thoughts and experiences. It is not, however, the kind of fear we might experience while alone in the dark. Rather, it is the kind of fear that might cause us to focus our lives on *it* rather than on the Lord, the kind of fear that might cause us to order our lives in a way that would betray a lack of trust in him. It is a fear that might cause us to lose perspective or to act as if something other than God himself has ultimate power over us.

This kind of fear may be familiar to some Christians. How often do Christians avoid communicating the truth of Christ out of fear that the response will bring about embarrassment or ridicule? How many Christians look at the future and act in a way that might ensure their own well-being, even at the expense or neglect of others? These and similar reactions come from a heart of fear, a heart all too anxious for self-preservation. This kind of fear can control us, and Peter's encouragement is that we should not allow it to do so.

THE LORD IS LORD

What is the paramount truth that we should keep in mind when our faith, and perhaps our very lives, are under attack? That, in essence, is the question with which Peter is faced. What do his persecuted and suffering readers need to remember?

With that in mind, Peter gives his readers one command. Verse 15 of chapter 3 is translated in different ways, but its force lies in the command to regard Christ the Lord as holy. To put it in one word, Peter's command is "Sanctify!"

The Greek word ordinarily translated *sanctify* (or *make holy*) is taken from a root from which we get other words in Scripture, such as "saint," "holy," "holiness," and "sanctification." Its primary meaning is "to set something apart" from something else. *Holiness,* for example, is not first and foremost a moral or ethical term, though it has definite ethical connotations. It is first of all a positional term. It refers to a particular position or placement of something. In the Old Testament, there were things like fire and crowns that were to be holy. These things obviously had no ethical or moral qualities. They were holy by virtue of their place or position—because of how they were used in Israel.

When Scripture refers to God as holy, it is telling us, first of all, that his position is fundamentally different from that which is unholy. God, as holy, is beyond, or above, everything else, since everything else is unholy in comparison to him. This is an important part of Peter's message. In chapter 1 he says:

> But as he who called you is holy, you also be holy in all your conduct, since it is written, "You shall be holy, for I am holy." (vv. 15–16)

Peter's admonition here is that Christians, like their heavenly Father, are to be separate from the things of this world, to distance themselves from those things that are contrary to his perfect character. This distancing is not necessarily spatial. It is impossible to live entirely apart from the world. The "distance" in view, rather, is positional. We are to be like God in *his* holiness.

This will, without question, have definite moral or ethical consequences. It means that we will look and act in ways that will make us different from that which is unholy. But the emphasis here is that we should *be* different because we *are* different. We are, as the Authorized Version says, "a peculiar people" (1 Peter 2:9). God has changed us to make us peculiar. We belong to him; he is our Father. Therefore, we are to bear the family resemblance. Because we are a peculiar people, we are to live peculiarly; we are to live as people who are positioned differently from all that is unholy. Our position in this world is that of citizens of a heavenly kingdom, an eternal family.

Peter's command in verse 15 is to sanctify (we could say "holify," if English would allow) Christ as Lord in our hearts. As some translations have it, we are to "set Christ apart as Lord" in our hearts. The emphasis in the original Greek is on the word "Lord"; it is the first word in the clause. Whenever a sentence is constructed that way, the writer is telling us what his emphasis is. So, given the actual word order, the passage reads something like "As Lord set apart Christ. . . ." Why does Peter give this command, and why is he emphasizing lordship?

Many of us have lived through and participated in national, state, and local elections of various kinds. At times, we may have a candidate that we think is equipped to make things better. Or, conversely, we may be convinced that a particular candidate, if elected, would do nothing but harm. We may even decide to volunteer our time in order to get a certain candidate elected, or to work against a candidate. Again, because we are "people of the senses," it can be easy to begin to act as if everything for good or ill rides on that particular candidate, or on that particular governing body. If the wrong candidate is in fact elected to office, we may begin to believe that there is no longer any hope for us or for our country. If "our" candidate gets in, we may be fooled into thinking that all will be right with the world, at least for the next few years.

Peter was writing to Christians who were living in a situation in which they were surely tempted to think that all hope was lost. He was writing to Christians who were despised by the government. They were living under conditions that were much more hostile than most of us could imagine. The battle was not merely a clash of ideologies. These Christians were likely facing death for their faith. They were living under conditions in which the emperor was executing many of their number. Their leader was not simply weak in economic policies or foreign affairs; he was not simply immoral and lacking in character. How quickly might we lose perspective if someone were to come to our house, and, by order of the commander-in-chief, put one of our loved ones to death because of our faith? We would certainly be afraid, and we would be tempted to think that, since the power of life and death was in the emperor's hands, *ultimate* power was in his hands as well.

The Christians during that time were tempted to think that the emperor had all the power. Surely one who holds your life in his hands is a powerful man, even if his power is put to wrong use. It was tempting to think that the emperor was in control and that God was not listening. It was tempting to think, as Peter himself had no doubt at one time thought (Mark 4:35ff.), that the Lord of creation was asleep while the storms raged all around.

The first thing that Christians need to burn into their hearts in these situations is that Christ, and Christ alone, is the true emperor; he alone is Lord. The first thing we need to have firmly established in our minds is that, as the early church confessed, "Jesus is Lord"—and no one else is. When fears set in and threaten to take over our lives, Peter is saying, even when everything around us looks gloomy, this is the first thing you must do: Set Christ apart as Lord.

We may think, in the face of such persecution, that "giving in" would relieve the pressure. And it may, for a time. But Peter is reminding his readers that their responsibility is to be faithful to the true king, the King of all kings. They are to obey him first of all.

Recall that Peter here is thinking of Isaiah 8. Interestingly, though, in Isaiah we are told that it is the "Lord Sabaoth," the Lord of hosts, who is to be set apart. Isaiah is reminding the Lord's people in that passage that, even if Assyria descends on Israel, God in heaven is the Lord of hosts. He is the captain of all the armies, and no one has power to tear down or to build up unless he receives it from the King of kings (see Joshua 5:13–15 and John 19:11).

Peter changes the designation here from "Lord Sabaoth" to "Christ as Lord." In that change, he is simply reminding his readers that Christ the Lord is Lord Sabaoth; he is the Lord of hosts. He is the commander of the armies of God and, in the end, the battle is his. The governments rest on *his* shoulders (Isaiah 9:6).

There would be no reason to defend the faith, to communicate the gospel, to aspire to holiness, if Christ were not the Lord. If Christ were not the Lord, then something or someone else would be. That "something else" would always have the power to undo or resist or erase whatever we did that was good. But since Christ *is* the Lord, no amount of opposition can ever thwart his good purposes. No resistance can stop the influence of obedience to his commands. Because Christ reigns, obedience to him is never frustrated.

Peter knew that the hearts of these Christians were no doubt at times filled with fear. They were afraid of the cruel abuse of power that the government was wielding. They were afraid for their very lives. Fear had gripped their hearts. When that happens, it is difficult to remain faithful. So Peter's command is, in effect, to set that fear aside and to set Christ apart as Lord in their hearts. In other words, Peter is telling them to "replace" the fear that grips them with the firm faith that Christ is in charge. They are to set *Christ,* not *fear,* apart as Lord of their hearts.

It is on this imperative, this command to sanctify Christ as Lord, that the rest of our defending and commending depends. It is our first priority to set Christ apart as Lord in our hearts. We must have the full assurance that he alone rules, and that the "powers that be," no matter how ruthless, rule in subjection to his sovereign lordship (Romans 13:1ff.).

This is how we should train ourselves to think. To set Christ apart as Lord in our hearts is to set him apart as Lord in a way that causes us to think differently. It causes us to think differently about the things around us. Because we know him as Lord, we know also that no one has ultimate power over body and soul except Christ himself.

DEFENDING THE KING

Jesus Christ is the King; we are his servants. As servants, we have the great privilege of defending his crown. We do that when we communicate to his enemies that he alone is Lord.

With Christ set apart as Lord in our hearts, we are to be ready, at any time, to give an answer. The Greek word translated "to give an answer" is interesting for a number of reasons. First, there can be little doubt that Peter had his Lord's warning from Luke 21, particularly verse 14, in mind as he wrote. Notice the similarity of Christ's warning in Luke 21:12–14 with the situation of those to whom Peter wrote:

> But before all this they will lay their hands on you and persecute you, delivering you up to the synagogues and prisons, and you will be brought before kings and gov-

ernors for my name's sake. This will be your opportunity to bear witness. Settle it therefore in your minds
not to meditate beforehand how to answer. . . .

In verse 14, Luke refers to that which is "in your minds." The
word translated "mind" is actually the Greek word *kardia,*
which is just as easily translated (as it is in some versions) "heart."
Notice that Peter refers to the heart in 1 Peter 3:15.

It is also striking that the root of the word translated "answer" in Luke 21:14 is also the root of a word used by Peter. No
doubt Peter was there when Christ gave this warning, and no
doubt he is remembering his Lord's own words as he writes.

The root of the similar words used in Luke 21:14 (translated as "answer") and 1 Peter 3:15 (translated as "give an answer") is the Greek word *apologia.* It is from that word that we
get our English word *apologetics.* As we said earlier, *apologetics*
means, generally, a "defense," or an "answer," to a particular
charge or challenge. It is a legal word, used often in a court-
room setting. It carries the idea of setting forth a response to an
accusation. Thus, when we speak of apologetics, we are talking about defending and commending the Christian faith in the
face of challenges and attacks that come our way.

The force of what Peter is saying here is striking. It is particularly striking because what Peter is saying is really what the
Lord himself is saying. He is telling us that, as Christians, we
are always to be ready to defend the faith. He is telling us that
a part of our Christian responsibility, as strangers in a strange
world, as those who will suffer, is to be people who respond bib-
lically to charges that come against us because of our commitment to Christ. The force and scope of Peter's command, then,
is that, in setting Christ apart as Lord, we are also, all of us, to
be apologists.

This may be surprising news, particularly to those who have just learned what an apologist is. But the passage is clear. Peter writes to Christians who are in a strange land. He tells them that at least a part of their response as "foreigners" is to be prepared to give an answer when their faith is challenged. Peter does not say that apologetics is reserved exclusively for the professionals.

There may be a need for those who are trained specifically in apologetics (I hope there is!). But the focus here is on every Christian; every Christian is to be ready to give an answer. When we find ourselves in hostile circumstances, we are to be people who are already prepared. We should have already prepared ourselves to give an answer. We are not to think first of all of passing the question on to the pastor or professional apologist. We ourselves must be ready.

What is the context of the answer that we are to give? It is, says Peter, that we are to give an answer to anyone who asks for a reason. The Greek word that Peter uses here, translated "reason," is *logos*. It could mean something like "logic"—not, of course, logic in its formal or symbolic sense, but logic in the sense of a consistent rationale, or ground, for our belief.

Some of the charges that were brought against Christians in the early church were (1) atheism, because they refused to worship the pagan gods, (2) cannibalism, because they spoke of eating flesh and drinking blood, and (3) incest, because "brother" and "sister" seemed to be married to each other. Peter is telling us that Christians must be prepared to give a consistent rationale or explanation in reply to such charges.

Those same charges do not seem to plague us now. But other charges have come. Christians are charged with being narrow-minded, irrelevant, prideful, and fanatical. It may certainly be true that we, in our sinfulness, act in such ways at times. But the charges against us often attack the very truth we believe, rather than our own character. It is those charges that we should be prepared to answer.

We must be prepared to see why these accusations are leveled against us, and we must be prepared to give the rationale and ground for our faith in Christ. If, for example, we believe that Jesus Christ is the only way to the Father, we may in fact be, in that sense, narrow-minded. But we must be able to say why we think the way we do and why we cannot think otherwise.

We are to give the logic, or reason, for the hope that is within us. I remember seeing a bumper sticker once that read, "I've given up hope and I feel much better." It is a humorous bumper sticker in some ways, but its humor is embedded in its tragic honesty. Someone could feel better by giving up hope only if that hope was hope in nothing at all—hope in hope. That kind of hope is empty; it has no real object. As an empty hope, it brings no real benefits. It brings nothing but confusion and anxiety, when faced squarely. So, it is better to give up that kind of hope than to hang on to it.

Christians alone have true hope. We hope, not in hope, but in Christ. Peter is alluding here again to the "problem" of invisibility. As Paul reminds us, hope in an object that is seen is no hope at all (Romans 8:24). But the hope that we have, while recognizing that its object is invisible, is nonetheless grounded in the one who himself has promised to come back and take us to our, and his, eternal home. Peter tells us here that we are to respond to the challenges that come by giving the "logic" of our hope.

GIVE WHAT YOU COMMAND

Augustine was one of the most influential theologians in all of church history. He was one of the first to write about his life in the light of his Christian experiences. In his *Confessions,* Augustine offered prayers to God about his life and his struggle to be an obedient child of God. One of the most memorable prayers in that work is this: "Lord, give what you command, and command what you will."

What Augustine is praying is profound in its simplicity. He is not praying that God would require less of him. He is praying that God would give him the resources he needs to fulfill all of God's commands. God may certainly "command what he will," but Augustine asks him also to "give what he commands."

The Lord commands his people to give an answer, to respond with a rationale for their hope. In commanding us to meet the challenges that come, he does not leave us without the resources we need to carry out that command. He gives us what we need, and all that we need, in his Word. Paul reminds the young pastor Timothy of this:

> All Scripture is breathed out by God and profitable for teaching, for reproof, for correction, and for training in righteousness, that the man of God may be competent, *equipped for every good work.* (2 Timothy 3:16–17)

This is no doubt a familiar passage to most Christians. But its truth bears emphasizing. After Paul tells Timothy what Scripture is useful for, he gives him the goal to reach. Scripture is to be used so that the Christian may be competent for every good work. The word "competent" may also be translated as "fully equipped."

This means that Scripture can equip us with everything that we will need to answer our challengers. It is perfectly sufficient for such a task; indeed, it was intended by God, in part at least, for that very purpose. So we need not fear that challenges will come to which we have no answer. Scripture provides us with the answers we need to properly and obediently defend and commend the Christian faith.

This does not mean, however, that we will have *all* the answers. It may be that certain questions will come that God has not been pleased to answer in a way that satisfies the inquisitor. Or it may be that we have not mastered a certain teaching of the Bible well enough to answer a particular question.

The Lord's command here is not that we acquire omniscience. It is a command to be ready for the challenges that come to us. While we will not, and should never claim to, have all the answers, at least part of our response at times is that we know the One who does. Part of our answer, then, is communicating to our challengers that knowing God in Christ makes all the difference. In knowing him, we come to trust and rely on the only one who does have all the answers.

BLESSED ARE THE MEEK

Much of what it means to be prepared to give an answer has to do with understanding the Bible and its implications. It means thinking through the truths of Scripture in a way that brings out those truths for today's questions. In that way, we learn, not just what Scripture says, as necessary as that is, but what it means in particular situations. It may help us at times to ask ourselves, as we are reading Scripture, just what it is that this truth means for our generation or for a specific situation that we have in mind.

Conversely, when we meet challenges to the Christian faith, whether in something we have read or seen, or in a conversation we have had, it is often beneficial to jot those challenges down and to have them handy when we read Scripture. We will likely be surprised at how the Lord anticipated in his Word the substance of every challenge.

Peter not only commands *that* we defend the faith, but also tells us *how* the faith is to be defended. He uses two significant words to describe how we should carry out our defense. He says first of all that our defense should be with "gentleness." Think of the intensity of the persecution that Christians must have been enduring when Peter wrote these words. How hard would it be, when faced with one's tormentor, to answer with gentleness? How easy would it be to fight fire with fire, to answer the persecutor in kind?

Peter remembers the attitude his Savior had. When Jesus was being challenged, he was gentle. Peter knew, because he had seen firsthand, the gentleness of Christ. Peter knew that the one who was truly unjustly accused, the one who would have had a legitimate reason to answer harshly because of the gross injustice he was having to endure, himself answered his accusers with gentleness and meekness (2 Corinthians 10:1). So, Peter is telling us here to have that attitude in ourselves which was also in Christ. He is telling us to live as Christ lived, even when the attacks and charges come against us.

We are also to be "respectful." The Greek word translated as "respect" is the word often translated as "fear." It is interesting that Peter uses this word, since he has just told his readers not to fear their persecutors. Now he says to answer them with "fear." The context is all-important in determining what Peter means by this second use of the word *fear*.

Many translators rightly translate this word here as "reverence" or "respect." That is what Peter means here. We are to respect those who persecute us; we are to treat them, though they are our enemies in the faith—better yet, *because* they are our enemies in the faith—with the respect due one who is made in the image of God. Or, to put it into the context of Isaiah 8, we are not to fear men, but to fear God. In fearing God, we will respect his creation, even those who set themselves against him.

This is a tall order. It is, without doubt, the hardest thing that we are required to do as we face our accusers. It is relatively easy to set our minds to understanding Scripture in order to be prepared to give an answer. It is even relatively easy, once we have done that, to give an answer. What is difficult is to give an answer that will imitate, and thereby glorify, our Savior. But that is the task set before us by the Spirit himself in his Word. And if it is required of us, God will give, and has given, the means for us to do it. In fact, unless he provides the means, it will not be accomplished. It can only be accomplished in him.

It seems that Christians have much to learn in this regard. Our natural reaction when confronted, or when persecuted, or when we are trying to fight back as "underdogs," is to lash out against our opponents more harshly than they did against us. Our first inclination, oftentimes, is to outdo their belligerence, to scream louder or to fight harder. But Christ, who had the authority of heaven and earth behind him, was not interested in a power struggle (John 19:11). He was not intent on showing "the powers that be" who was really in charge. He answered his accusers gently and with humility.

That is our model. That is our challenge. That is our privilege—to follow Christ, even when the attacks come, and to answer with gentleness and respect.

Since we are strangers and aliens in this world, both our final kingdom and our King are invisible. Much of what we see is opposing him. Our response is to prepare ourselves. It is important to remember that we are required to understand his Word in the light of objections and questions that may come our way.

In order to begin thinking in this way, we will need not only to read Scripture, as necessary as that is, but also to meditate on what we have read. We will need to develop the habit of thinking through the implications and applications of the truth that is presented to us in God's Word. This may take some effort that is initially foreign to us. Developing a habit is always more difficult than maintaining one. If we can develop the habit of asking questions, probing questions, about what we have read in Scripture, then we may find that meditating on what we read in Scripture will eventually come more naturally to us.

Peter does not require us to know every answer to every question that might come. He requires us to be ready. The only way to be ready is to know the Scriptures, and to know them in such a way that we will be able to bring out their truths when the challenges and objections come our way.

Having made ourselves ready to give an answer, we will find ourselves meeting objections to the Christian faith, whether face-to-face or in things we see or read. We may still be surprised that people would raise certain objections. Nevertheless, we will be ready to give an answer. More importantly, we will be obedient to the one who has commissioned us for that task. And we will be imitating our Savior.

So what do we say to Marv when he is convinced that Freud is right? We might begin by asking Marv why he trusts what Freud says, rather than what Christ has said. He may respond that he is not sure what Christ has said. That is the kind of response that gives us an opening to share the gospel. Or we may ask him to tell us in some detail what Freud has said and why. We may ask him to defend Freud's view of the world, of people, of the human mind. It may be that Marv is simply searching and would be just as happy to give up Freud, if something else were offered.

Whatever Marv's response, whether we have read Freud or not, the Scripture is sufficient to give us the answers Marv needs. His trust in Freud is just one more way to distrust Christ. So we defend the truth of the gospel, seeking to turn Marv away from Freud and to our faithful Savior, who, unlike Freud, shed his blood so that the likes of Marv, and of us, could truly live. *That* truth is worth defending—and telling!

> Ye servants of God, your Master proclaim,
> And publish abroad his wonderful Name;
> The Name, all-victorious, of Jesus extol;
> His kingdom is glorious, and rules over all.
>   (Charles Wesley)

DIGGING DEEPER

1. Why do suffering and persecution tend to give us focus in the Christian life? Is it possible to get that focus without suffering? How?

2. In what ways does our identity as people who are "in Christ" make a difference in our defending and commending the faith?

3. Name four current events that should be understood in the context of Christ's lordship. How would that perspective influence your defense of the faith?

4. If someone asked you to say in three sentences why you believe Christianity to be true, what would you say? What objections can you anticipate to your statements? How would you answer them?

5. Why are gentleness and respect so difficult for many of us to develop? How can we begin to develop them *before* we are confronted?

BEWARE THE IDES OF MARCH

IT WAS MARCH 15, sometimes called "the ides of March." It was a day like any other day. But, as the soothsayer ominously reminded Julius Caesar, the emperor, the day was not yet over.

Cassius and the Roman leaders were afraid that Caesar's power was going to his head. Too much power for Caesar meant too little power for them. So they plotted to assassinate him. They even convinced Caesar's good friend, Brutus, to join them in the assassination plot. And before the ides of March was over, Caesar was murdered. The tragedy of his death was that his friend had conspired to kill him.

At least since the time of Shakespeare, and probably because of the power of many of his plays (*Julius Caesar, Romeo and Juliet*), the word *tragedy* has taken on a more specific meaning. It seems that the philosopher Aristotle gave the word its original meaning. For him, tragedy was a more general category that had to do simply with the drama of a presentation. As the concept has evolved, however, it has most often been associated with the notion of a surprising and unexpected evil. In *Julius Caesar,*

Beloved, although I was very eager to write to you about our common salvation, I found it necessary to write appealing to you to contend for the faith that was once for all delivered to the saints. —Jude 1:3

the tragedy of Caesar's death is expressed by Shakespeare in those three famous Latin words, "Et tu, Brute?" The tragedy of the play is centered in the fact that Brutus, the friend of Caesar, became one of those who sought his demise. The surprise in the phrase says it all: "You, too, Brutus?" Caesar's own close friend had betrayed him.

The book of Jude is a tragedy of sorts. It reminds us that there will be times when those who are closest to us will seek our demise. It reminds us that often in our own households, even in the church of Jesus Christ, we should "beware the ides of March" because the day is not yet over. It reminds us to encourage one another, as we see the Day drawing near (Hebrews 10:25). It reminds us that the faith is to be defended and commended even *to* and *among* the Lord's people.

The church father Origen said of the book of Jude that it "was small, but filled with a vigorous vocabulary."[1] That vigorous vocabulary is used by Jude to motivate his readers, and us, to contend for the faith. Although small in size, Jude packs a powerful apologetic punch.

The similarities between the book of Jude and 2 Peter (particularly the second chapter) are unmistakable. There can be little doubt that there is a dependence of one epistle on the other. Although we have less information on Jude's intended audi-

---

1. Jerome H. Neyrey, *2 Peter, Jude,* Anchor Bible (Doubleday: New York, 1993), 27.

ence than we have on Peter's, their concerns were largely the same. They were both concerned to encourage the church to defend itself against those who would seek to subvert or undermine its ministry. The purpose in each book is, therefore, an apologetic one. Jude writes to a church, or group of churches, to help them defend themselves against a specific attack on the gospel, an attack that is taking place within the church itself.

AN INSIDE JOB

We will focus our attention in this chapter on Jude, verse 3:

> Beloved, although I was very eager to write to you about our common salvation, I found it necessary to write appealing to you to contend for the faith that was once for all delivered to the saints.

Jude had a purpose in writing this epistle. Originally, he had wanted to write a letter of encouragement. He had wanted to emphasize the unity that he and his original readers shared together in Jesus Christ. But because of the situation facing them, he decided to write to them, not about their unity in the faith, but rather about defending the faith that unified them. This short epistle turns out to be an encouragement, then, to do apologetics.

The apologetics that they were encouraged to practice, however, had a focus that may, at first glance, surprise us. Since apologetics has to do with defending and commending the faith against attacks and charges that come our way, one might think that it is aimed only at those who are outside the church of Jesus Christ. In one sense, that is true. The opposition that is pictured in Scripture is typically an opposition between the world and the church (see, for example, Jesus' prayer in John 17:14–16). In principle, the battle lines are clearly drawn between the church and the world.

We know, however, that what is true in principle is not always true in practice. Such is the case in the church of Jesus Christ. This should come as no surprise to us. Jesus himself prepared us for this. In the parable of the wheat and the weeds, he told us exactly what would happen in the church. He told us that "while his men were sleeping," the enemy would come in and sow weeds among the wheat (Matthew 13:25). When the wheat seeds take root and begin to grow, so do the weeds.

Of course, our natural reaction to this, as servants of Christ, is to rid the field of all the weeds. But Jesus said that this was not the responsibility of the servants. If they tried to do that, some wheat might get destroyed as well. We are to "let both grow together until the harvest" (Matthew 13:30). In other words, the "weeding out" process is to be left to the Lord of the harvest in his own perfect time.

Although we cannot completely rid the church of its "weeds," it is not the case that the weeds will always be unrecognizable. How then are we to approach the "weeds" that infiltrate the church? Jude helps us to answer that question. The Christians to whom Jude writes had experienced exactly what Jesus foretold in the parable. There were those who had "crept in unnoticed" among them (Jude 4). They had come into the church while Christians were asleep. It is not exactly clear who these people were. It does seem, given the language Jude uses, that his readers knew at least something about this group and their teachings. But they had escaped the notice of Jude's audience; they had slipped in secretly.

It is not only that they had slipped in secretly, but also that they had begun to influence some believers in the church as well. Some had apparently begun to doubt the faith, and others were dangerously close to falling away from it altogether (vv. 22–23). So the ones who had sneaked in were also carrying on covert operations among these Christians to subvert and destroy, if possible, the faith on which the church was built. How could such a thing happen?

It is fascinating to try to trace the reasons why and how Christian teachings or Christian churches or Christian institutions "go bad." Although specific situations always have specific characteristics, the general pattern seems to be just what Jude lays out here. Rarely do good things, or good and holy institutions, regress through obvious and unambiguous means. Rather, influences and ideas seem to move in slowly, at times undetectably slowly. Once in, however, in many cases, they continue, just as slowly and subtly, to wear down the essential character of their target.

This kind of erosion rarely takes place openly. It rarely resembles flood waters inundating a house. It happens rather like a slowly dripping faucet in the basement of a house, quietly, though methodically, inflicting serious damage on the foundation of the house until it crumbles from its own hidden rot.

This is one of the things that we learn from Genesis 3. Remember how we are introduced to the Evil One who seduces Eve? We're not told that Satan entered the garden in a straightforward way to destroy all that was good. Rather, we're told that "the serpent was more crafty than any other beast of the field that the LORD God had made" (Genesis 3:1).

The very first thing that the Lord wants us to know about the introduction of evil on the earth is that the serpent was the

most crafty of beasts (or, as the Authorized Version has it, the
serpent was "more subtle" than the others). This should warn
us that the most serious and despicable of evils will likely come
to us in casual and apparently harmless attire.

We see that further in the serpent's approach to Eve. There
is no way to know how Eve might have responded if the serpent had simply come to her and said, "Choose whom you will
serve—Satan or the Lord God!" The point, however, is that he
did not come to her in that way. Rather, he came with a question—one that perhaps, on the surface, looked like a simple request for information. "He said to the woman, 'Did God actually say, "You shall not eat of any tree in the garden"?'" (3:1).

No doubt Satan knew exactly what God had said. His question was not one of simple curiosity. He was after much more
than information. The way in which he got his answer is instructive because it was so subtle. The serpent was able, in asking the question, to manipulate Eve's own concerns. By asking
the question in the way that he did, he was able to focus her concern on his deception. He was able to get Eve to question God's
command to her. First came the question, then the blatant opposition. Only after getting Eve "on his wavelength," so to
speak, was he able to present to her the "other" option: "You
will not surely die" (3:4).

This is how attacks and assaults operate within the Christian church, within Christian teaching and Christian institutions. They tend to work, subtly and almost undetectably, to
bring us into their context of concern. They begin with subtle
questions or "concerns." Underneath such questions lies a denial of biblical truth. If we begin to entertain those questions,
we can, almost unconsciously, be involved in the same denial.
Once there, such questions, with their subtle denials, can begin

to "drip" into the foundation of our most cherished commitments in order to make those commitments, if possible, rot away.

Jude had discovered that the faucet was dripping among these churches, and it was dripping in a way that was taking its toll on the Lord's people. It was threatening the foundation of the church itself. So he wrote to instruct them about the nature of the opposition and to tell them what they should do about it.

THE ENEMY WITHIN

Before focusing on what Jude asks his readers to do in this situation, it would be helpful to look more specifically at the opposition these churches were facing. Jude's description of the enemies who have made their way into the church is illuminating. He does not describe them as merely worldly people.

Paul's list of sins in Romans 1:29–30, for example, is a list of typical worldly sins, the sins of crass unbelief. He describes people who are wicked, greedy, malicious, etc. But Jude describes the sin of those who have slipped into the church in much different terms. He speaks of their sin in terms that show both the subtlety and the tension that arise when opposition comes from within the church, rather than from outside. These are people who have "walked in the way of Cain." They have "abandoned themselves for the sake of gain to Balaam's error and perished in Korah's rebellion" (v. 11).

These examples are taken from the Old Testament. Jude refers his readers to well-known sins that occurred in the history of the Lord's people. And we should not miss the point that these sins occurred *in the context of the Lord's people*. These sins are infamous among the Lord's people because they were carried out "in the church," as it were.

Jude does not use more obvious illustrations, such as the Assyrians or the Philistines in their attempts to conquer and subvert Israel. The peculiar thing about the sins that Jude mentions is that they were not just worldly sins. Rather, they were sins that served in some way to undermine the work of the Lord among his own people. Jude uses these three illustrations to remind his readers, as the hymn writer reminds us, that there are "false sons within the pale" of the church.

Those infiltrating the church or churches to which Jude writes are not merely foreigners who come in to conquer and rule. These troublemakers are craftier than that. They know something about "the tradition" of the churches they seek to subvert. They may come in from the outside, but they are shrewd operators on the inside. They know the tradition and can "speak the language." Thus, they are even more dangerous than someone who would come in forcefully from without. We should note Jude's emphasis in these examples.

Cain, of course, was the first murderer. He did not murder an enemy. He murdered his own brother, motivated by an angry heart. Cain was not an outsider to the Lord's people. He belonged to the "first family." He was the firstborn of the family of Adam. By all rights, the lineage of the Lord's people should have been traced through him.

But instead, he became the father of those who rebel against the Lord (Genesis 4:25–26; 1 John 3:12). Although Cain was initially identified with the Lord's people, he acted in a way that would, but for God's provision, destroy them. By his very act of sin, he both separated himself from the people of God and left them without a "father." If God had not provided Seth, the people of God would not have continued.

In choosing the way of Cain, the intruders desired, according to Jude, to reverse the direction of the church. They wanted to murder, as it were, the lineage of Jesus Christ, and therefore to move it toward its own destruction. The way of Cain was the way of murder, murder from within the house of the Lord.

Jude's reference to Balaam, no doubt, refers to Moses' condemnation of his actions in Numbers 31:16. It was because of Balaam's counsel that Israel was almost destroyed. There was in Jude's day an idea that Balaam did what he did for money. He was found with the Midianites when he was killed (Numbers 31:6–8). Some held that he was among foreigners then to collect his reward. Jude uses that idea to communicate to these Christians that the false teachers among them are concerned only for their personal gain. They are, Jude says, those who "feast with you without fear, looking after themselves" (v. 12). Just as Balaam was responsible for the death of thousands of Israelites for profit, so these false teachers are concerned only about their own profit, no matter how many of the Lord's people they might lead astray in the process. In using this example, Jude was attempting to show that these false teachers, though pretending to be with them, were far from the discipleship that Christ himself had taught, a discipleship of service and of self-denial.

The reference to Korah would have been particularly stunning to Jude's readers (see Numbers 16 and 26). This is probably why Jude referred to Korah last. His reference is stunning in a number of ways.

First of all, Korah was a priest of Israel. He was supposed to be dedicated to the continuation of Israel's devotion to her

Lord. But he used his status as a priest to rebel against the order and structure that God had set up in Israel. To put it in New Testament terms, Korah used his leadership position in the church in order to exalt himself and his own agenda. He was not content to keep his place. He wanted to take over other positions of leadership and to bring the Lord's people down with him.

Jude's use of Korah is striking also because he does not simply refer to Korah's rebellion. He wants to remind his readers of the *result* of Korah's rebellion. He wants to remind them of Korah's judgment. In calling to their attention the judgment of Korah, Jude is not simply reminding his readers of Korah's sin, comparing it to the sin of the false teachers who have come in. He is reminding them of Korah's end as well—an end, he is implying, that will come to all of those who follow in Korah's steps.

This theme of judgment is a significant part of Jude's letter (see, especially, vv. 14–15). This is a reminder, not only that it is wrong to follow those who go astray, but also that following them brings an eternity of punishment. Korah was the Old Testament symbol of that punishment (Numbers 16:33).

It is also interesting that Jude uses a word to describe Korah's rebellion that refers primarily, not to Korah's actions, but to his words. He writes in this way, it seems, to call to our attention the dangerous and seductive influence that arguments can have on us. It was Korah's disputation, his debate, that lured others in Israel to him, and thus to their own destruction. This word is used only three other times in the New Testament, all in the book of Hebrews. It is used in Hebrews 12:3, where it applies to the opposition that Christ himself had to endure:

> Consider him who endured from sinners such *hostility* [translated as "rebellion" in Jude 11] against himself, so that you may not grow weary or fainthearted.

The hostility in view here in Hebrews reached its climax at the Cross. The crucifixion of Jesus was the ultimate attempt to destroy God's plan and thereby his people also. The rebellion of Korah was a type of that same opposition. It was an opposition, an argument, against the authority of the church in the Old Testament. In that way, it was an argument against Christ himself. So also, Jude is saying, are the rebellious disputes of the false teachers.

These three illustrations in the Old Testament highlight Jude's concern about the false teachers. It would be hard to overemphasize the problem that Jude is addressing in his letter. The problem is that the church has been infiltrated by those who oppose the gospel. They have come into the church and live among the Christians.

In professing to be a part of the church, they hope to lead others astray. They are like some of the Israelites who, though delivered from Egypt, were nevertheless destroyed (v. 5). They are like the angels who, though created good by the Lord himself, nevertheless rebelled and fell from their created position (v. 6). They are like the inhabitants of Sodom and Gomorrah (v. 7). All of these serve to underline the dangerous situation in which these churches find themselves as Jude writes. The weeds are in full bloom and will choke the life out of any wheat that is there, unless the Lord intervenes through his faithful servants.

How, then, should Christians respond?

THE GOOD FIGHT

Jude's purpose in writing was to encourage and prompt his readers to action. The enemies within, as we have seen, were both subtle and dangerous. In Jude's mind, there was one thing that the Christians had to do. They had to fight.

Fight is not one of those words that we normally associate with the Christian faith. That is as it should be. Christianity is concerned with reconciliation. Its message is one of "good news," and part of its goal is to bring together people from every tribe, language, people, and nation (Revelation 5:9). These diverse people are meant, in the end, to be *one* kingdom and *as one* to worship and praise the King of kings and Lord of lords. Christianity's message is not, in the main, a message of division and strife, but one of unity and peace. We are called to maintain the unity of the Spirit in the bond of peace (Ephesians 4:3). Jesus Christ himself is called by Isaiah the "Prince of Peace" (Isaiah 9:6).

But there is another side to our faith that is necessary for us to remember as well. It is necessary because of the sinfulness that remains in the world until Christ returns. Remember what the Prince of Peace told the Twelve before he sent them out?

> Do not think that I have come to bring peace to the earth. I have not come to bring peace, but a sword. For I have come to set a man against his father, and a daughter against her mother, and a daughter-in-law against her mother-in-law. And a person's enemies will be those of his own household. (Matthew 10:34–36)

Why this note of tension? Why does Christ want us to understand that there will be this kind of opposition? This doesn't sound like peace; this sounds like division and discord.

These words can be difficult to understand. It seems obvious, though, that at least part of what Jesus is telling his disciples is that our commitment to follow him must be a "whole-souled" commitment. He is telling us here what he has told us elsewhere—that it is impossible to serve two masters. Any attempt to serve two masters will result in our hating the one and loving the other (Matthew 6:24).

Even very good things, things that we should rightly cherish, things that bring us joy and blessing, things like family relationships, must never take the position of "Master" in our lives. Once we choose to follow Christ, our ultimate allegiance cannot be placed anywhere else. Following Christ will mean letting go of anything else that we previously followed—even if that includes family members!

But the language that Jesus uses here is much stronger than that of mere allegiance. He speaks of enemies, war, and fighting. Christ himself was prepared to fight. As the Prince of Peace, he nevertheless came to bring a sword (Matthew 10:34).

It is worth remembering that the apostle Paul himself spoke about a fight. Toward the end of his life, as he wrote to counsel the young pastor Timothy, he reminded Timothy that he had fought the good fight (2 Timothy 4:7). That, perhaps, is the best way to think about the task to which Jude calls his readers. It is the best way for us to think about the apologetic task that we have as well. Although it may sound paradoxical, we are called to fight a "good" fight. This fight, as Paul says elsewhere, is the good fight *of faith* (1 Timothy 6:12). It could even be said that the *only* good fight is the good fight of faith. It is the fight that has its center and its focus in the Christian faith.

Jude calls his readers, and us with them, to fight the good fight. As we saw, Christ taught his disciples that "a person's enemies will be those of his own household." If that is true of our families, it is certainly true as well of the household of faith. Our enemies will sometimes live and work in the closest proximity to us—in our homes, perhaps, and even in the church of Jesus Christ.

So, says Jude in verse 3, we are to "contend" for the faith. The word translated "contend" is used nowhere else in the New Testament. It was commonly used elsewhere for either military combat or athletic contests. By using this word, Jude would have automatically called to his readers minds either a military battle or an athletic event. Both of these metaphors, the military and the athletic, are familiar ones in Scripture. Paul encourages Timothy to "share in suffering as a good *soldier* of Christ Jesus" (2 Timothy 2:3). He commands us elsewhere to *compete* in such a way as to win the prize (1 Corinthians 9:24).

The point of Jude's use of this word is to highlight the fact that these Christians must view themselves as being in the midst of a difficult battle or contest, *even in the midst of the church!* By their profession of faith, because they are following Christ, they are drafted into an army, so to speak, and it is time for them to exert great effort for the sake of this faith, to the glory of their Savior.

As we will see in the next chapter, our fight is most certainly not to be fought using the weapons of the world. The fight that we fight will only be a "good" fight if it has Christ, the Lord of hosts, as its captain. It must be carried out using only the weapons that our captain provides.

But the presence of these opposing forces within the church means that there is no time for ease and relaxation in the churches to which Jude writes. They are to protect that rich deposit that was given to them in the gospel. The way in which Jude describes this fight indicates how the spiritual war should be waged.

THE FAITHFUL FIGHT

If we followed the original word order of Jude's description of the faith in verse 3, it would read something like this: Contend for "the once-for-all-delivered-to-the-saints faith." There are three elements of this faith that Jude calls to our attention. We will look at those shortly, but first we need to understand what Jude means by *"the* faith."

Most of the time, when Scripture uses the word *faith,* it is referring to the faith that we have as a gift from God (Ephesians 2:8). Faith, in this context, is something internal.

The internal aspect of faith relates primarily to our activity. This is the way the New Testament uses the word most often. It can be little or great (compare Matthew 15:28 with 16:8). It moved the Savior to heal (see Mark 2:5; 5:34). It can be weak or strong (Romans 4:19–20). When Scripture speaks of faith in this way, it is referring to that gift of God as it is applied and exercised by us. This faith is applied and exercised, initially, at our conversion, and it continues to be exercised by us in our Christian walk (which Scripture calls our sanctification).

It is this aspect of faith of which the Westminster Confession so eloquently speaks:

> By this faith, a Christian believes to be true whatsoever
> is revealed in the Word, for the authority of God him-
> self speaking therein; and acts differently upon that
> which each particular passage thereof contains; yield-
> ing obedience to the commands, trembling at the threat-
> enings, and embracing the promises of God for this life,
> and that which is to come. But the principal acts of sav-
> ing faith are accepting, receiving, and resting upon
> Christ alone for justification, sanctification, and eter-
> nal life, by virtue of the covenant of grace. (14.2)

Scripture emphasizes this kind of faith because it is such a crucial and important part of our Christian experience.

The aspect of faith to which Jude refers, however, is not primarily the internal aspect of our faith. The faith to which Jude
refers is not the faith that we have in Christ, or the weak or
strong faith that is in us; rather, it is something that is outside
of us. It is *the* faith. And while it is certainly related to our internal faith, it is a different thing altogether.

While we may believe *the* faith, and certainly Jude's readers did believe it, it was not their own personal belief that they
were to fight for. It was something that was external to them,
something that was there even if they didn't believe it. (Of
course, if they didn't believe it, they would have no reason to
fight for it.) They had become committed to this faith, and it
was this external faith that they were to fight for.

It is important to remember this for a couple of reasons.
First of all, when we are contending for our faith, we are not,
in the first place, fighting for something that we have, but might
lose. It is not the faith that God has given to us that is the point
of contention. Rather, it is the truth of Scripture. More specifically, it is those truths that make up the gospel. Second, because

what we contend for is the gospel, we need to be clear about just what that gospel is. We need to know what *the* faith is, since we're called to fight for it.

We find this external faith mentioned also in the book of Acts. In Acts 6:7 we're told that "the number of the disciples multiplied greatly in Jerusalem, and a great many of the priests became obedient to *the faith*." Here the faith that is spoken of is a kind of standard, a measuring rod, to which Christians became obedient. Elsewhere, the faith is something to which Christians are to remain true (Acts 14:22), and in which they are to be strengthened (Acts 16:5).

When Scripture speaks of "the faith," it is referring to a body of truths or doctrines we come to believe when we trust in Christ. While it is not referring to my belief itself, it is related to my belief in that I have committed myself to these truths. The faith is, in one sense, what I must be willing to die for. It includes the very gospel that saves us (Romans 1:16). It is *the faith* that we come to *believe*.

"The faith" was a way of speaking about the truths that Christians believed. It was called the *faith,* at least in part, because it referred to *what* they believed. There are certain truths that every Christian must believe in order to be a Christian. Although just believing those things to be truth will not make one a Christian, one cannot be a Christian without such belief.

That body of truth is called *the faith*. It includes things like the truth of Scripture, God's existence, and Christ's incarnation, death, and resurrection. It includes the fact that God has saved his people, that Christ will come again, etc. These truths are crucial for the life of the church. Without these truths, the church has no way to help and minister to those who want to grow in grace.

This is why Christians from early on in the history of the church have set out creeds and confessions as expressions of what they believe. These are designed, not only to tell others what is believed, but also to remind us of what we believe. They are designed to help us see the unity, harmony, depth, and riches of the diversity of God's written revelation to his people.

Many churches still recite the Apostle's Creed in their worship services. If we recite that creed, we say that we believe, for example, that God is the Father Almighty, the Creator of heaven and earth, that Jesus Christ is his only Son and our Lord, that he was conceived by the Virgin Mary, and that he suffered under Pontius Pilate. We are not saying something about our personal exercise of faith—whether it is weak or strong, for example. Rather, we are saying something about the truth content of our belief. We are declaring *the* faith. It is this for which Jude's audience was to contend. And it is this for which we are to contend.

We have no way of knowing exactly what "the faith" consisted of when Jude wrote his epistle. The earliest Christian creed of which we are aware consisted of the affirmation "Jesus is Lord" (1 Corinthians 12:3). The Apostle's Creed had not yet been written when Jude wrote. But we should not underestimate the ability of Christians in the first century to articulate their faith. Although the Nicene Creed was centuries from being written, there is little question that, when Jude wrote, Christ was seen as fully God. The first confession—"Jesus is Lord"—says as much.

Jude was particularly concerned with the way in which false teachers had perverted the grace of God. Some commentators refer to these false teachers as "antinomians," which means that they were "against law." Generally, the term refers to people who interpret the grace of God as a license to sin. They see no real use for the law of God.

The relationship of grace to obedience is one of the trickiest and most controversial teachings in the history of the church. It should not escape our notice, therefore, that Jude seems to have known enough about the grace of God and its relationship to obedience to know that there were some in the church who were twisting and manipulating those truths to their own wicked ends.

So, even though we do not have the text of any creed or confession of faith that may have been used during this time, there can be little question that Jude understood enough about God's grace to recognize its counterfeits—and that he expected his readers to know the same. "The faith," then, for Jude and his readers, likely contained most of what orthodox Christianity has always held to be true. It may not have been articulated as precisely, or in the words to which we are accustomed, but it must have been there nevertheless. It was *this* faith, *the* faith, for which the Christians were to vigorously contend.

ALL FOR ONE AND ONCE FOR ALL

Jude calls this faith the "once-for-all-delivered-to-the-saints" faith. What does he mean by "once for all"? At least part of what he means is that there is a certain completeness to what they believe. This completeness has been guided and directed by God's own plan and providence in history.

When Adam and Eve were in the garden, God's revelation to them was "once for all." That is, what they received from the Lord was complete; they didn't need any more revelation than what he gave them. Nor would they get any more than they needed at that time in history. The same was true for Abraham, and for Israel, and for the Christians who lived in the first century.

Nothing was to be added to or taken away from the revelation that they had from the Lord (see Deuteronomy 4:2; Revelation 22:18–19). It was given by God once for all. To add to his commands, or to take away from what he had revealed, would be to deny its character as revelation given once and for all. And it would be to deny its sufficiency. God has always given exactly what is needed—no more and no less.

There is a completeness about the revelation of the first century, however, that marks it off from all the other revelation that God has given in history. No doubt Jude understood this. Since Christ had come and completed his work, the time of God's special revelation to his people was over. As the author to the Hebrews puts it, "Long ago, at many times and in many ways, God spoke to our fathers by the prophets, but *in these last days he has spoken to us by his Son*" (Hebrews 1:1). Whether or not Jude knew that he himself was writing Scripture is unknown. But he did seem to understand that the revelation that was given in Christ was, like Christ's own work, completed.

The revelation given in Christ was complete because of the work that Christ had done. Jude was referring, essentially, to the gospel. The gospel, the good news, was founded on Jesus Christ's completed work—his life, death, resurrection, and baptizing in the Holy Spirit at Pentecost. These events had occurred once for all. Jude knew that. There was a completeness to them that, if supplemented or diminished, would only pervert their truth. Christ had come, he had died, he had risen from the dead, he had ascended into heaven, he had sat down at the right hand of God, he had baptized Christians with the Spirit at Pentecost.

These events all took place with a view to our redemption, our salvation. And they were all complete.

These events would not be repeated because there was no need to repeat them. They were Christ's work, and his work was finished. Jude understood that the faith that was to be defended could only be properly defended if it was wrapped up in the once-for-all finished work of Christ. If there was more revelation to come, then it just might be that the intruders in the church deserved a hearing. But Christ's work was complete. Any attempt to pervert, subvert, supplement, or subtract from that work should provoke a good fight; it should cause us to take up our spiritual armor and do battle.

Of course, the writing down of this revelation in Christ was in process when Jude was writing. Not only was it in process with respect to what Jude himself was writing, but there was more to be written from others as well. It is likely that Jude had in mind the words that Jesus had spoken to his disciples concerning the Holy Spirit. It was better that he go away, Jesus had told them in the Upper Room, because if he did not go, the Holy Spirit would not come (John 16:7).

Part of the ministry of the Spirit among the disciples was to guide them "into all the truth" (John 16:13). Peter understood that Paul himself had written under the inspiration of the Holy Spirit; as a result, he called Paul's writings "Scripture" (2 Peter 3:16). Given the close connection between Jude and 2 Peter, Jude probably understood that the Spirit who had come at Pentecost was inspiring the writing down of this complete, once-for-all revelation.

This is an important point for those who must defend and commend the faith. The faith that we defend is a faith that culminated in Jesus Christ. It is a faith that understands that God's revelation is complete in Christ. It is a faith that recognizes the necessity of revelation itself, which is Jude's own emphasis.

S P E C I A L   D E L I V E R Y

The "once-for-all-delivered-to-the-saints" faith is not only once for all, but also delivered. This points us to the source of the faith that we defend. The faith is delivered, or handed down, to us. The word that Jude uses here highlights the fact that our faith is revealed. It is a faith that has been given to us by God himself. It is not something that we have invented on our own. It is not a faith that has its source in Jude, or in the apostles, or in some human intellect. It has its source in God alone:

> "What no eye has seen, nor ear heard, nor the heart of man imagined, what God has prepared for those who love him"—these things God has revealed to us through the Spirit. (1 Corinthians 2:9–10)

The faith that we have, those truths that we are to defend, are truths given to us by God. Since they have God as their source and origin, they are quite literally "heavenly" truths. We have a heavenly faith that has never been, nor could ever be, produced by a merely human mind. Our faith comes from the mind of God.

This would have made the false teachers in the churches uncomfortable. They were "grumblers, malcontents, following their own sinful desires; . . . loud-mouthed boasters, showing favoritism to gain advantage" (Jude 16). If Christians were to defend the faith against such teachers, they needed to know that what they were defending in no way originated with them, or with Jude, or even with any of the other apostles. What they were defending originated with God alone; it was given by his Spirit.

So the authority that stood behind their defense of the faith was God alone. A part of their defense must have been (as ours must be) "Thus says the Lord." The false teachers, the "loud-mouthed boasters," would have flinched at such humility (because what we say is God's word, not ours), combined with such authority from the Lord.

Any defense of Christianity, then, must be based on divine revelation. If we are asked or challenged to give a reason for our faith, we dare not think that we believe things that originated with us. We dare not give the impression that we believe what we believe because we are smarter or more perceptive than those who do not believe. What we have, we have by the grace of God. What we believe, we believe not because eye has seen, or because ear has heard, or because heart has imagined, but because, and only because, God has revealed it to us by his Spirit. It is to the revelation of God that we must go if we are to defend the faith. It is there that the faith is given; it is in that revelation that it is explained. It was delivered to us, and by God's grace we have received it.

FOR ALL THE SAINTS

Some have seen in the book of Jude a refutation of the religious movement called Gnosticism. In its varied forms, Gnosticism held, among other things, that its truth could be discovered or understood only by those who were "in the know." The word *gnostic* comes from the Greek word for "knowledge." It was an exclusive religion, in that sense. It excluded anyone who did not, or could not, obtain the proper knowledge.

Christianity is an exclusive religion too, in one sense. All who have not trusted in Christ are excluded from its life-changing, life-giving benefits. But those who have trusted him are, simply by virtue of that trust, a part of his eternal kingdom. There are, of course, differences within the Christian church. There are some who are gifted in mercy, for example, or in preaching, or in knowledge. But those gifts assume that one already *is* a Christian. They are not "tickets" that get us in.

Jude is reminding his readers that this faith for which we are to fight, even within the church, this "once-for-all-given-to-the-saints" faith, was and is given *to the saints*. We noted in the last chapter that the word Peter uses in 1 Peter 3:15 for "sanctify" ("regard as holy," ESV) is a word that has to do with holiness. The word that Jude uses here for "saints" is taken from the same word. It could easily be translated as "those who are set apart." The faith is delivered to all those who are set apart. The theological term for that is "sanctified." Jude is telling his readers that God has given this faith, once for all, to the sanctified body of Christ, to those who are set apart as holy. Sanctification means to be, as well as to become, holy.

The Bible uses the term *sanctification* in at least two different ways. It speaks of us as in need of sanctification. We need to become holy in Christ (see John 17:7; Romans 6:22; 1 Thessalonians 4:3; 5:23). Sanctification in this sense is a process of growing more and more into the image of Jesus Christ (Romans 8:29). This is a process which reaches its completion at our glorification in Christ on the Last Day.

But the Bible also speaks of our sanctification as something that is an accomplished fact. It is something that has already taken place in us. Paul's first letter to the Corinthians is instructive in this regard. He addresses that letter "to those sanctified in Christ Jesus" (1 Corinthians 1:2). And lest we think that he is referring only to a select few within that church (especially given all of the problems at Corinth that he has to address), Paul goes on to remind them that it is because of God that they are in Christ Jesus.

Since we are in Christ Jesus, he has become "our wisdom and our righteousness and sanctification and redemption" (v. 30). Being *in* Christ brings the benefit of holiness, or sanctification, in him. Later Paul reminds these Corinthians that, even though they still struggle with the *process* of sanctification (one need only read the letter to see that), their lives have been changed by the work of Christ in their hearts.

After listing a number of life-dominating sins, Paul says to them, "And such were some of you. But you were washed, you were sanctified, you were justified in the name of the Lord Jesus Christ and by the Spirit of our God" (1 Corinthians 6:11). Paul is telling them here that in Christ, by his Spirit, they were sanctified. They were set apart in Christ, brought into his kingdom, and saved from sin for his glory.

When Jude speaks of "the saints," then, he is not referring only to a select few. He is not saying that only those who have reached a certain level of holiness have had the faith once for all delivered to them. Rather, he is telling his readers, and us, that this faith has been given to us all. It has been given to all who are set apart in Christ—who are, by definition, saints. To be in Christ is to be "sainted." To be sainted is to have the faith. To have the faith carries with it the responsibility of defending and commending it. Apologetics is for all the saints.

Jude wrote to encourage Christians to contend for the faith—within the confines of the church itself. How might someone go about doing that? The primary way to contend for the faith is to explain and expound the reality and truth of the Bible itself. Since the false teachers in Jude's day were perverting the grace of God, the Christians to whom he was writing needed to put God's grace back into its proper gospel context. They needed to be able to argue that a grace that leads to immorality is opposed to the faith, that it is not a part of the grace of the gospel at all. They needed to show that genuine grace is expressed in obedient gratitude, in holiness, and in faithfulness to that gospel.

The faith for which we are earnestly to contend is the faith that is given to us all. It is given to us all in God's special revelation, the Scriptures. We have now received, not only Jude's letter, but the entire canon of Scripture. That gives us an obligation to defend the faith, to contend for it, even, if need be, in the context of the church of Jesus Christ. We are obliged to fight the good fight of the faith; we must press the truth-claims of Christianity on unbelieving ideas and actions, even if they are found within the walls of the church itself.

As we are called to "beware the ides of March," we are put on alert that there may be some in our own midst who not only begin to deny the faith, but also would like for us to follow them. Like Brutus with Caesar, they would like nothing more than to betray us. Misery loves company, and the more the merrier. We are to prepare ourselves to do battle with some who are close to us.

The only way to do this, as we saw in the last chapter, is to know the Scriptures. If we know what grace is, even as Jude knew, then we will be able to tell when someone comes into the church with "a different gospel" (Galatians 1:6–9). We are called by Jude to defend that gospel, that faith, which the Lord himself has delivered to his people, once in Christ and for all time.

Digging Deeper

1. What are some ways to guard against attacks on the faith from within the church of Jesus Christ?

2. Are you familiar with any situation (person or institution) where there has been a decline of the faith? Can you trace the decline? Could it have been avoided? How could apologetics have helped in such situations?

3. Why is it that arguments often seem more powerful to deceive us than behavior? What does this say about apologetics? What does it say about the human heart?

4. What makes the Christian fight a *good* fight? How can we avoid turning the good fight into a bad fight?

5. What are the top ten elements of the faith? How do you know which elements are the most important?

6. How does the completeness of revelation help us in defending and commending the faith?

3

THE STEALTH ATTACK

THE SECOND LETTER to the Corinthians is the most auto-biographical of Paul's letters. We learn more in this epistle about Paul's life and heart than in any other. Paul thought it was neces-sary to say so much about himself because his life and ministry had come under attack in the church at Corinth. Just as we saw in Jude, there were those who had infiltrated the church at Corinth from the outside. They had come in with the express purpose of undermining Paul's ministry and exalting their own. The seri-ousness of their deceit can be seen in Paul's description of them:

> For such men are false apostles, deceitful workmen, dis-guising themselves as apostles of Christ. And no won-der, for even Satan disguises himself as an angel of light. So it is no surprise if his servants, also, disguise them-selves as servants of righteousness. Their end will cor-respond to their deeds. (2 Corinthians 11:13–15)

> *For though we walk in the flesh, we are not waging war according to the flesh. For the weapons of our warfare are not of the flesh but have divine power to destroy strongholds. We destroy arguments and every lofty opinion raised against the knowledge of God, and take every thought captive to obey Christ.* —2 Corinthians 10:3–5

Whatever these intruders taught, Paul uses strong language to describe them, even identifying them as Satan's own servants.

When the opposition is strong, the issue often centers on the notion of authority. One of Paul's primary purposes in writing this letter was to show the Corinthian Christians that he carried out his ministry as an apostle of Jesus Christ. As an apostle, his ministry was to carry out Christ's work here on earth. An apostolic ministry was unique in the history of the church. It was a ministry that carried with it the full authority of Christ.

Those who have put their trust in Christ have a similar responsibility today. No one has apostolic authority anymore; there are no apostles who receive or write down the word of the Lord. Because we have the word of God written in our Bibles, however, we can come to those who are opposed to the cause of Christ with his full authority. As it was in Paul's case, so it often is today—the issue is rooted in a disagreement over ultimate authority. The word of God is our ultimate authority. We should be so convinced of this truth that we are not afraid to say it confidently and boldly (with reverence and respect) as we stand ready to give an answer.

The problem that Paul had to address was apologetic at its root. It was not simply that his reputation was on the line. If that had been the only problem, he would probably have simply suffered the abuse. He was well aware of the mistreatment that would come to him as an apostle (1 Corinthians 4:13). It was not his reputation that was of great concern to him; rather, it was the truth of the gospel itself that was at stake.

These "servants of Satan" had come in, not simply to discredit Paul's leadership, but to convince the Corinthians to reject his message. These intruders were trying to deceive the Christians at Corinth into thinking that Paul's leadership was weak, and therefore that his gospel was too.

So Paul declares:

> For if someone comes and proclaims another Jesus than the one we proclaimed, or if you receive a different spirit from the one you received, or if you accept a different gospel from the one you accepted, you put up with it readily enough. (2 Corinthians 11:4)

There are two serious problems that are addressed here. The first is that the intruders are preaching another gospel, another Jesus, and are proclaiming another spirit. The second, just as serious, is that the Corinthians are "putting up" with it. They are tolerating this false ministry within the confines of the church!

It should come as no surprise to us, then, that Paul sets out to defend himself. In defending himself, he is defending his apostolic ministry. It was that ministry that founded the church of Corinth (see Acts 18), and Paul wants to ensure that this church will persevere in the gospel, rather than pervert it.

CHRISTLIKE CONFRONTATION

There is no question that the last four chapters of 2 Corinthians take on a distinctly different tone than the previous chapters. Commentators have debated the reason for this. Whatever the reason, however, Paul begins in chapter 10 to take a strong apologetic stand against the intruders. He begins chapter 10 by laying out his line of defense, which will be in sharp contrast to the attacks of his opponents.

Paul begins with a striking measure of personal intensity. The first verse of chapter 10 could more literally read, "I, Paul, I myself, I appeal to you. . . ." There is much repetition here, and it is here for the sake of emphasis. The emphasis is placed on his apostolic ministry. He appeals in this verse to his apostolic authority and speaks against those who were seeking to discredit or undermine it. He wants them to have no doubts about the authority of the ministry that he has been given in Christ.

This should serve as a pattern to us when we are presented with an opportunity to defend the faith. Of course, we have no apostolic authority. We are not given, as Paul was, the apostolic task of setting the infallible agenda for Christ's church until he returns. But we do come as those who have been commissioned by Christ. Paul reminds the Corinthians in chapter 5 that he comes to them as an ambassador of Christ, appealing to them to be reconciled to God.

We should think of ourselves, to some extent, as ambassadors as well. God has committed to us, through Christ and his apostles, the ministry and message of reconciliation (2 Corinthians 5:18–19). When we come with this message, as Paul did, it is as though God were "making his appeal through us" (v. 20). Our defense of Christianity, then, comes with God's authority, not our own. If it came with our own, it would carry only as much weight as we could muster. Even on our best days, our defense would be insufficient.

But since our message comes with God's own authority—since, that is, we come as his representatives, armed with the truth of God as our belt (Ephesians 6:14)—it carries the power and dominion and authority of God himself with it. When we speak the truth, we speak his truth. Our message is not something that we have invented; it is not something that we have thought up. It is something that we have been given. It carries the authority of its infallible source.

What difference does that make, particularly if the one to whom we speak does not recognize that authority? I can remember occasions in my family when, in order to settle a dispute between my brother and me, I would run to my father. Once he gave his judgment on the matter, I could go with the freedom and confidence of his authority to my brother and give the verdict.

The first thing that we must get firmly embedded in our souls is that when we meet the opposition, when we are called upon to "give an answer," the answer that we give, if it is God's answer, can be given with the freedom and confidence that it comes from our heavenly Father, the final and ultimate judge. We can know, beyond a shadow of a doubt, that what we say is exactly the truth of the matter. We can be confident that our message comes with the fullest authority imaginable.

Of course, there were times when, even if I came with my father's judgment, my brother would not listen. At least two things were true when that happened. First, my brother knew where he stood with my father at that point. He was not ignorant of what he should do or what his responsibility was. Second, if he steadfastly refused to abide by my father's judgment, he would eventually feel the effects of that refusal.

So it is when we come to those outside of Christ with his message. It may very well be that the message we bring—that message of reconciliation that Paul sets out to the Corinthians—will be roundly rejected. But those who reject this message, those who deny our defense, will have heard clearly where they stand with Christ. And, should they steadfastly reject his message, they will feel the effects of that rejection for eternity.

The only way to come with this kind of authority is, as Paul says in 2 Corinthians 10:1, with "the meekness and gentleness of Christ." It is noteworthy that the attitude with which we come is highlighted for us again, just as it was in 1 Peter 3:17. Paul begins this way because of the accusations that the false teachers have lodged against him. Paul was accused of carrying an attitude of false humility to the Corinthian church. And, said Paul's accusers, if his attitude is false, his message must be false too. They were trying desperately to convince the Corinthians that Paul could not be trusted.

Paul does not merely reject their accusations; he reminds his readers that his humility is patterned after that of his Savior. He is not simply saying, "I *really am* humble"; rather, he is connecting himself and his ministry again with the life and ministry of Christ himself.

Perhaps one of the most difficult things about the Christian life, and particularly about apologetics, is the balance of authority and gentleness that is required if it is to be practiced obediently. It is easy to move too far to one side or the other. We can become so excited about the authority that we have in the truth that God has given to us that our only goal is to set it forth. But such zeal may be anything but meek and gentle. It can communicate that the truth that we have is ours because of who we are, rather than because of what Christ has done.

On the other hand, we may be so impressed by the gentleness and meekness of Christ that we will do anything to avoid a confrontation. But that, too, can give the wrong impression. It can give the impression that the gospel, and particularly the Christ of the gospel, is not concerned with faith and repentance. It can leave others thinking that God is indifferent to sin. It can give the mistaken impression that everyone is accepted by, or acceptable to, God.

In the first chapter of his gospel, John tells us much about Christ as the Son of God. In verse 14, he tells us that the Word, this Logos, who was with God and was God (John 1:1), became flesh and dwelt among us. John then recounts his experience on the Mount of Transfiguration, where he, James, and Peter saw the glory of Christ revealed (see Matthew 17:1ff.). In thinking of the glory of Christ, John summarizes who Christ is. He is one who is "full of grace and truth."

This, at least in part, is what it means to be Christlike. If the glory of Christ is described by John as a fullness of grace and truth, then to glorify Christ, to "show him off," as it were, means to show both grace and truth together. If we are to glorify God, we must be full of both grace and truth, just like Christ.

We will glorify him when, and only when, our truth is seasoned with grace, and when our grace is combined with his truth. This cannot be accomplished on our own. It must be a work of the Spirit. This is not something that we are able to do in and of ourselves. It is a part, albeit a crucial part, of our being conformed more and more to Christ's holy image.

Paul is about to enlist warfare terminology and imagery in order to defend the gospel. That kind of imagery in our day can call up ideas of a *jihad,* a holy war, in which whole races are hated and killed in the name of religion. Paul knew that his language had to be strong; the accusations against him and his message were strong and were winning converts. He could not use strong language without first reminding the Corinthians that he was coming to them with Christ's own meekness and gentleness. That is something we must never forget in our defense of the Christian faith. Like Christ, we must strive to be "full of grace and truth" in our defense of this marvelous faith.

D E M O L I T I O N

We demolish arguments. That is one of the things that characterizes the ministry of the apostle Paul. As we saw in chapter 1, it is one of the things that must characterize our own lives and ministries as well. We know that there is, and always will be, hostility to the Christian faith. We also know that anything that opposes Christianity is, by that very act, false. We know this, not because we are smarter than others, but because of what God's grace has done in our lives.

We should note in this passage the strong offensive language that Paul uses. It is one thing to defend the faith against attacks. If we use the analogy of a sporting contest, the team on defense is trying to stop the other team from advancing. That is a significant and crucial part of apologetics. We pray and work as God uses us to stop the advance of the enemy, Satan himself. But we must also be offensive. We must also take up our weapons and march against the enemy. Of course, in being offensive we are also being defensive. But the offensive "team" is more active than the defensive team. The offensive team is determined to advance.

One example of this might help to illustrate it. Christians are often told that the problem of evil shows that their faith is not rational. It is often argued, in other words, that the existence of a good, all-knowing, all-powerful God is simply inconsistent with the abundance of evil we have in the world. We are told, then, that we should give up on our belief in such a God.

Answers to this challenge can be either more offensive or more defensive. A more defensive answer would try to show that the argument itself carries little weight. It would set the argument out in such a way that it would appear itself to have serious problems. In that way, it would stop the advance of the argument. A more offensive approach, however, would respond to the problem, not just to the argument, to help the challenger begin to think about the problem in a different, Christian way. Offensive apologetics, then, offers the Christian way of thinking and doing as a part of its approach.

Paul's concern in this passage is that, in our defense, we be offensive as well. Paul knew that the intruders at Corinth were building up their own cause by tearing down his ministry. He knew that an attack on his ministry was an attack on the truth of the gospel itself. So he wrote the last four chapters of 2 Corinthians to respond to those attacks. The first six verses of chapter 10 form the general introduction to what he will say in the rest of the letter. He wants his readers to know that his response will demolish their arguments.

It seems likely that the arguments and the approach taken by these false teachers originated with a group of philosophers known as Sophists. The name *Sophist* is taken from the Greek word for "wisdom." There may have been a certain genuineness to the Sophists when their sect started, but by now there was nothing admirable about them.

Among the Greek philosophers, for example, the Sophists were the first to charge a fee for the dispensing of their wisdom. Prior to that, the advancement of knowledge was seen as so important in itself that it was thought to be unseemly to do it for monetary reward. The Sophists, however, were literally "in it for the money."

As a general rule, the Sophists had little concern for truth. They moved from place to place, in Greece and elsewhere, showing people how to win their arguments, regardless of their merits. They were not concerned about the truth, but rather about how best to argue. They had a high regard for disputation. They would develop arguments for any and every position, and sell those arguments to interested buyers.

It is from the Sophists that we get our word *sophistry*. *Sophistry* refers to a false argument set forth for the sake of personal gain. The Greek philosopher Aristotle described the Sophists in exactly those terms.

Since the Sophists were interested only in the art of disputation, their expertise was in the use of rhetorical devices like irony, paradox, sarcasm, and subversion. Their approach to argument was to demean their opponents by attacking their integrity. Because they had no concern for truth, they had no time for real thinking. Whatever had to be accomplished, they thought, could be accomplished by debating technique and by argument.

There is little doubt that Paul had this kind of sophistry in mind when he wrote 2 Corinthians. He also had it in mind when he wrote 1 Corinthians:

Where is the one who is wise? Where is the scribe? Where is the debater of this age? Has not God made foolish the wisdom of the world? (1 Corinthians 1:20)

The "wisdom" of the Sophists was made foolish by God, by the gospel from God that Paul preached in Corinth.

Because the Sophists were concerned merely about debate, the best Sophist was the best orator, whether or not he was arguing anything that was truthful. It may not be surprising, then, that even in Paul's time the Sophists were drawn more and more to politics! The charge against Paul was that he was not a good debater: "For they say, 'His letters are weighty and strong, but his bodily presence is weak, and his speech of no account'" (2 Corinthians 10:10). Not having the Sophists' powerful debating skills, Paul was not as impressive as they were.

Since the Sophists had originated the practice of charging for their services, they had begun to think that their services were actually worth the money! Conversely, they also began to think (and to argue) that those who did not charge a fee for their oratory services obviously had nothing of any value to say. They attacked Paul for not charging for his ministry—"Or did I commit a sin in humbling myself so that you might be exalted, because I preached God's gospel to you free of charge?" (11:7). The false teachers had actually convinced some in the Corinthian church that eloquence was the only virtue that they needed; it alone was the key to happiness and success. They had also convinced them that those who were not as eloquent must be wrong.

Since entertainment has become our primary pastime, we no longer place a premium on oratory skills. In Paul's time, however, and particularly at Corinth, the primary pastime was debate. It has been said that in Corinth there was a philosopher on every corner.

The false teachers sought to attack Paul's character. This kind of argument is sometimes called an *ad hominem* argument.

This Latin term literally means "to the man." An *ad hominem* argument often seeks to be convincing by attacking the character of the opponent. It does not seek to win the argument on the merits of the argument itself. It tries, rather, to tear down the other debater in order to make one's own argument look better. The Sophists were masters of this kind of argument, and the "false apostles" in Corinth were following in their steps.

Although Paul is describing his own apostolic ministry in 2 Corinthians 10:4–5, that does not mean that what he says is only descriptive. He is, as an apostle of Christ, showing us how we should respond to attacks on our faith. If Paul was ready to demolish arguments, we must be ready as well. In other words, Paul meant for his statement to be applied by his readers to their own situation.

We know that is true because Paul uses expressions in verses 4 and 5 that are taken from at least two different biblical passages. His notion of demolishing strongholds, in verse 4, is akin to the Septuagint version (the Greek translation of the Old Testament) of Proverbs 21:22. There we're told, "A wise man scales the city of the mighty and brings down the stronghold in which they trust." Paul, no doubt, has this passage in mind as he thinks of the sophistry of his attackers.

He also knows that some in the Corinthian church would have made this connection. By using this terminology and by referring them to the book of Proverbs, he is telling them that true wisdom consists of demolishing strongholds in which the mighty trust.

It is not true wisdom simply to erect an argument, whether true or false, as Paul's opponents had done. Rather, the wisdom that is from above must, at the right time, tear down the fortresses that are falsely erected. Christians who seek to be wise must also "pull down the strongholds" when the need arises.

Paul uses terminology that is close to terminology that others used of the Sophists. By doing so, he gets the attention of his challengers. He tells those "deceitful workmen" that their facades are going to fall. They may be intent on developing and selling arguments to refute and destroy Paul's ministry, and thus the church in Corinth itself, but Paul is putting the church on notice that he himself will demolish the arguments advanced against him.

This is the "good fight of faith" that we spoke about in the last chapter. It is the responsibility of every Christian to defend and commend the gospel. That defense is a process of demolition. It is a demolition of the arguments presented against Christianity. As we have seen, we have in God's Word all that we need to accomplish that task. And, as we have said, it is a task to which God calls each of us.

Paul's word for "arguments" is directed specifically against his opponents' appeal to authority. They were attempting to establish themselves as authorities in the church solely because of their own expertise, their own intellectual power. So Paul reminds us that the arguments of these intruders are only as authoritative as the intruders themselves. The authority for what they said, therefore, was merely in their own ideas and reasonings. It was, quite literally, a figment of their imagination. So Paul is saying that he is going to demolish the false authority on which these false apostles rested.

This will be the case whenever we engage in apologetics. Apologetics, in many ways, is simply a battle over authorities. It involves making plain just where we stand, or better, where we rest, with regard to what we claim. It also involves encouraging our opponents to make plain where they rest their own case. The issue of authority is always primary.

The idea that Paul presents in the next clause tells us a good bit about arguments he was opposing. The clause could be translated as "every high thing raised up against the knowledge of God." While Paul is alluding to the sinful pride of his attackers, he is also pointing out that their sophistry makes a pretense of sophistication and erudition. Their arguments may have sounded lofty and substantial, and may have been intimidating because of their vocabulary, but they were really, in the end, just opinions. They had no more authority behind them than did the Sophists themselves.

Paul is pointing out, as well, that these arguments are not just verbal debates. They are arguments that, if believed, will have eternal, and eternally damaging, consequences. Although they carry no authority, they can cleverly lead people to reject the gospel itself. They are dangerous because they are so subtly subversive of the gospel. They are, as a matter of fact, arguments that are raised up against the very knowledge of God itself.

The history of much of the Western intellectual tradition is full of such arguments. This may be one of the reasons why many Christians have chosen to stay well away from that tradition. It can be intimidating and can make us feel intellectually inferior as Christians.

We should recognize two things, however. First, we should understand the seriousness of the arguments themselves. If they are raised up against the knowledge of God, then they can be destructive to any and all who adopt them. Second, we should begin to understand that Christianity does have answers to these arguments. Even if we are unfamiliar with the precise terminology and technicality of the arguments themselves, once we grasp the question that they are designed to answer, our understanding of Scripture can begin to supply the answer.

Apologetics includes, to a large extent, a kind of "mind-set." Much of what we do in order to be "always ready" is to burn the truth of Scripture so firmly into our hearts that we see its truth in the midst of everything else around us. If we can set our minds that way, then we will not be intimidated by other "lofty things" that come along our path. We need to see that there is nothing more lofty than the truth of Scripture in all its richness and fullness. We need to be convinced again that "the whole counsel of God" is the only high and lofty thing worth believing. We need to understand that the only place for a human being to rest is in the knowledge of God and of Jesus Christ.

There is a passage in C. S. Lewis's book *The Silver Chair* that serves as a helpful picture of the importance of setting our minds in the proper place. One of the children, Jill, is being sent from the mountaintop down into Narnia by Aslan, the lion. Before she is sent, Aslan says to her:

> But, first, remember, remember, remember the Signs. Say them to yourself when you wake in the morning and when you lie down at night, and when you wake in the middle of the night. And whatever strange things may happen to you, let nothing turn your mind from following the Signs. And secondly, I give you a warning. Here on the mountain I have spoken to you clearly: I will not often do so down in Narnia. Here on the mountain, the air is clear and your mind is clear; as you drop down into Narnia, the air will thicken. Take great care that it does not confuse your mind. And the Signs which you have learned here will not look at all as you

expect them to look, when you meet them there. That
is why it is so important to know them by heart and pay
no attention to appearances. Remember the Signs and
believe the Signs. Nothing else matters. And now,
Daughter of Eve, farewell—.[1]

We are to read Scripture, to remember it, to say it to ourselves
when we "wake in the morning and when we lie down at night,
and when we wake in the middle of the night." We are to let
nothing turn our minds from following what God has said,
from viewing the world in the way he has described it to us.
Things do, often, appear differently "in the world" from the
way that they are presented to us in Scripture. We must remember the Scriptures.

Few of us will have the kind of experiences that Paul had.
Few of us will find ourselves at the center of a major contro-
versy over the truth of the gospel. But we all have been, or will
be, in situations where the truth of the gospel is under attack.
It may be a subtle, "friendly" attack. It may come in the form
of a "simple" request for information (Genesis 3:1). When it
comes, we are to be ready to demolish the arguments.

Paul is not ashamed to characterize his situation as war. An
attack on the Christian faith is a declaration of war. It is not a
declaration of war simply against us. Paul knew that. It is a declaration of war against the truth of Christianity, and thus against
the one who is the truth (John 14:6). So, given the meekness and
gentleness of Christ, what else do we need with which to fight
this war, this good fight of faith?

1. C. S. Lewis, *The Silver Chair* (New York: Collier Books, 1953), 21.

STEALTH WEAPONS

"We destroy arguments" (2 Corinthians 10:4), but "we are not waging war according to the flesh" (v. 3). This is, perhaps, the most difficult thing for us to realize as we think about our duty to defend the faith. We do not wage war "according to the flesh," that is, "as the world does" (NIV). Paul says, "For though we walk in the flesh, we are not waging war according to the flesh" (v. 3). This translation helps us see what Paul is after.

In verse 3, Paul is answering the accusations that he mentions in verse 2. There are some in the church who are saying that Paul is "worldly," in the worst sense of that term. They are accusing him of being unspiritual, of living and moving comfortably with the things of this world, rather than with "spiritual" things. There is a false spirituality at Corinth that Paul has to address here. He has two responses.

First, he says, we *do* walk according to the flesh. Paul obviously does not mean to imply here that we walk according to the sin that remains in us (see Romans 6–7). Rather, he means to refute those within the church who define spirituality by its distance from everyday life. There are some who are saying that the way to be really spiritual is to avoid the mundane things of this life, to avoid the physical "stuff" of this world. Those who don't avoid such things, like Paul, are said to be fleshly, worldly.

Paul affirms that he does live and move *in* this world. It is not an unspiritual thing to be familiar with, and to walk among, the ways of this world. That does not automatically make one a "worldly" Christian. Paul uses the word *walk* in order to affirm that he, and we, must conduct our lives, go about our daily routines, within the context of this world. This is an essential part of Christ's own prayer, and God's own design, for his people (John 17:13–19).

But as we conduct our lives in this world, we do not *wage war* in a worldly, or fleshly, way. Paul has already alluded to this. No one who comes in "the meekness and gentleness of Christ" (2 Corinthians 10:1) can, at the same time, respond in a worldly way. But now he wants his readers to understand just how he proposes to destroy arguments. In the meekness and gentleness of Christ, Paul claims that this demolition is accomplished with weapons of divine power. What could Paul mean?

The Greek preposition translated "with" could be translated a number of ways, but all of them indicate that Paul's weapons derive their power, not from the world, but from God alone. Paul's discussion of warfare here is in many ways similar to his discussion in Ephesians 6:10–18. There Paul lays out for us just what weapons we are to use "in the strength of his might" (Ephesians 6:10). It may help us to look briefly at Paul's description there.

In Ephesians 6, Paul reminds us that the battle that we fight is not a fleshly battle. He means by that precisely what he means in 2 Corinthians 10. We must "walk in the flesh," that is, in this world, but our battle is not a worldly one. We do not use worldly means for worldly ends. Our battle is one of "other-worldly" power against "other-worldly" powers, of the Spiritual Authority against other spiritual authorities. Our battle is against the forces of evil in the heavenly realms. Even if we did use worldly weapons in this kind of battle, they would be to no effect. Bombs, guns, and canons are of no use against spiritual powers and authorities.

A spiritual battle requires spiritual weapons. So Paul tells us in Ephesians 6 how to arm ourselves in this kind of struggle. The weapons that he lists are familiar. We fight with truth, righteousness, the gospel of peace, faith, salvation, and the word of God. Of course, Paul describes each of these as a piece of our armor. They all serve to protect and defend us. It should not escape us, though, that each one of these weapons comes from God alone. They all carry with them the authority that God has.

Truth, righteousness, the gospel, faith, salvation, and the word of God are all weapons that could never be produced, built, controlled, or taken by us. They could only be created and given by God. He alone is the maker of these weapons. He alone can give them. When he gives them, they come with his full authority. Thus, there cannot be any stronger weapons to use. These are the weapons that give us what we need to be strong in the Lord and in his mighty power (Ephesians 6:10).

It is curious that Paul begins his list of armor in Ephesians 6 with the belt of truth and finishes it with the word of God. What could Paul mean by truth that is in some sense distinct from the word of God? At least part of what he must mean is that we are to come armed with a true understanding of the nature of the problems we confront and of the world. It means that we are to look at things in this world through the lens of Scripture. Then our "read" on the situation is informed by what is really the case. We need to see the world as it really is; we need to see it as what God says it is. This may sound easy, but a lack of scriptural vision has led to countless errors being made in defense of the gospel.

A scriptural vision, what we sometimes call a biblical worldview, is what Paul is referring to here as the belt of truth. That may be one of the most crucial weapons of all. It is the first weapon that Paul mentions. He mentions it first so that those who are armed for battle may have the proper military strategy. This is similar to what Peter wrote when he instructed us that we are to focus on the lordship of Christ first of all as we prepare for our defense.

For example, we are not to think that those who claim to have ultimate authority really possess such a thing. The Corinthians were not to think that the intruders really were apostles, or "super-apostles," as Paul calls them (2 Corinthians 12:11). We are to ask ourselves, as we engage in spiritual battle, What is the reality, the truth, of the situation? We are to send, so to speak, the military scout ahead to report back to us the "lay of the land." We are to be armed with the belt of truth, so that we might be equipped to fight with the sword of the Spirit.

These are our weapons in battle. It is easy, all too easy, for us to fight the world's battles in the world's way. This is a great temptation for us. We need only look at how we respond in other situations to see just how easy it is. One of the things that has struck my family and me is the difference in the day-to-day culture where we live now, compared to where we used to live. For example, in our former place of residence, there was a slower, more polite pace on the roads. Where we are now is anything but slow and polite. But what has struck us recently is how acculturated we have become in that regard. We seem to have picked up the bad habits of drivers here, almost unconsciously! Now we find ourselves battling on the road just like other drivers.

How much more is this the case as we "walk" in the world? Paul says we are not to fight that way. We are to take up arms from a different source and therefore fight in a different way. Our battle, the real battle, is against the powers and authorities in the heavenly places.

It is common knowledge among military commanders that the first priority of a military offensive is the element of surprise. If the enemy does not know the attack is coming, or does not know how or when it is coming, then the possibility of success increases dramatically. One of the most formidable military weapons developed in the United States is an airplane commonly called "the stealth bomber." The advantage of this weapon is that, despite its enormous size (with a wing span of fifty yards), it can hardly be detected by radar. It can fly into battle without the enemy ever knowing that it is coming.

The weapons that we are to use in our defense are "stealth weapons." We are to go into battle with invisible weapons, weapons with which the enemy is unfamiliar, weapons that will surprise him. When the enemy is surprised, he is much more prone either to defeat or to surrender. Spiritual weapons are our stealth weapons. While those attacking Christianity might expect us to respond in kind, we are encouraged by Paul to respond with weapons that only we can understand—truth, faith, righteousness, a spiritual sword. Our enemy will be surprised at these weapons. By God's grace and providence, he might even surrender to the gospel of grace.

PRISONERS OF WAR

Paul's final military allusion is in the statement that we "take every thought captive to obey Christ" (2 Corinthians 10:5). The verb translated "take captive" refers to a prisoner of war. Paul is in the battle of his life. He is at war, demolishing and destroying those things that are raised up, not against him alone, but against the very knowledge of God. Now Paul tells us that he is concerned, not simply to demolish those thoughts, those lofty things that have set themselves up against the knowledge of God, but to take them into captivity. He is concerned to make them prisoners of Jesus Christ.

This is a striking statement, particularly in our day and age, when we might think that thoughts are too abstract or unimportant to be concerned about. In one sense, Paul is tracing the problem at Corinth to the thinking of the Corinthians.

This should not surprise us. After his exposition of the gospel in Romans 1–11, Paul begins to discuss the application of that gospel in chapter 12 by telling us to be transformed. But just how are we to be transformed? When we hear the word *transformation,* perhaps our first inclination is to think of the way we live, of doing the right things. We may tend to think of the Christian life as a series of observable dos and don'ts. Those things are indeed important, and Scripture has much to say about them. But the first thing on Paul's mind when he begins to think about the transformation of our Christian lives is the renewal of the mind. This means that the way we think has much to do with the way we live.

This idea needs to be stressed again today in Christ's church. Because of technology's unprecedented access to our "private" life, we can convince ourselves that, as we surf the Internet or chat online, we are anonymous. This may explain the explosion of pornography and other immoral business on the World Wide Web. We may have fallen prey to the idea that God cares only about how we act "in public."

But this notion betrays an ignorance of biblical priorities. We are to be transformed, not by improving our public life, but by renewing our mind. We are to be changed into the image of Christ by changing our mind, first of all. When we do this, we realize that there is no distinction, in the eyes of God, between public lives and private lives. We are as fully in God's presence when we surf and chat on the computer as we are in church or at work. To focus on behavior to the neglect of the mind, in other words, will inevitably lead us into temptation.

We are to take every thought captive to obey Christ. We are not to be taken in by sophistry and things that purport to be wise. Our thinking is to be molded by the thinking of Scripture, so that when "lofty things" come our way—lofty things that are raised up against the knowledge of God—we can immediately recognize them as nothing more than so much hot air.

There will be lofty things to contend with in the world. The world, since the Fall, has never lacked for arguments aimed at undermining or destroying the Christian faith. It is impossible to learn them all; no one has the time to do that. What is possible is to begin to take every thought captive to obey Jesus Christ. Then, when those arguments come, those captive thoughts will be exactly what is needed to begin the demolition. And all this is to be done, of course, in the meekness and gentleness of Christ himself.

Our plan of attack is like that of a stealth bomber. We are to attack with weapons that are invisible to the natural eye, moving in with the sword of the Spirit, in order to pierce the hearts of our opponents, so that they too may, by God's grace, be taken captive to the King of kings.

> Make me a captive, Lord,
> And then I shall be free;
> Force me to render up my sword,
> And I shall conqu'ror be;
> I sink in life's alarms
> When by myself I stand;

Imprison me within thine arms,
And strong shall be my hand.
                    (George Matheson)

DIGGING DEEPER
1. Name five characteristics of an ambassador. How do these relate to being an ambassador of Christ?
2. Give an example of an *ad hominem* attack. What is the best way to respond to this kind of approach?
3. How do we develop a scriptural mind-set? What kinds of things try to draw us away from that mind-set?
4. How can you arm yourself with "the belt of truth"?
5. Why are thoughts so important in the spiritual battle?

4

THE GOOD WITH THE BAD

IN THE PREVIOUS CHAPTERS, we attempted to show the importance of apologetics in the life of the Christian. We focused our attention, first, on Peter's command to be ready to be apologists. Then we looked at two examples of apologetics, one from Jude and one from Paul. Jude showed us that apologetics is not just for those outside the church. At times it is also needed within the church. The example from 2 Corinthians showed that as well, but it also gave us some clues about how apologetics should be practiced. Paul set the apologetic parameters for us—we are to destroy arguments and take every thought captive to obey Christ. Just as Paul appealed to the Corinthians in "the meekness and gentleness of Christ," so we should exhibit those qualities in our defense of the faith.

We have seen that apologetics is a fight, a good fight—perhaps *the* good fight. Christians are to fight with the weapons that God provides, and do so in his power. In this war, there are two opposing sides. There are those who have put their trust in

> *For I am not ashamed of the gospel, for it is the power of God for salvation to everyone who believes, to the Jew first and also to the Greek. For in it the righteousness of God is revealed from faith for faith, as it is written, "The righteous shall live by faith."*
>
> *For the wrath of God is revealed from heaven against all ungodliness and unrighteousness of men, who by their unrighteousness suppress the truth. —Romans 1:16–18*

Christ and who long to serve him as their commander-in-chief, and there are those who have not trusted Christ, but whose trust is in themselves and their own devices.

As we have said, both sides can exist within the church. But this does not change the fact that there are two sides to this war. Even when the enemy crosses over into friendly territory, he is still the enemy. Indeed, that is when he becomes the most dangerous.

One of the more difficult aspects of apologetics is the fact that we are required to deal with unbelief in its various forms and expressions. When we study theology, or exegesis, we have the luxury of remaining within the confines of Christianity, for the most part. But unbelief is part of the purview of apologetics in a way that it is not in theology *per se*.

This has not always been recognized in apologetics. There are times when we are tempted to think that, because we are convinced of a particular argument, everyone else will be also. Or, there are times when we think that certain things are "obviously" true to anyone, without realizing that unbelief is designed to miss the obvious. We can at times be tempted to think that an argument that is compelling to us as Christians will be compelling to everyone. But because of sin, that is not the case.

The passage with which we are working in this chapter and the next could be the most crucial passage for a biblical understanding of apologetics. It outlines for us specific areas of unbelief that we could never know by mere observation or by innate principles. It gives us God's perspective on unbelief. So it is an essential passage if we want to understand to whom it is we speak as we seek to defend the faith.

For that reason, we need to spend some time looking through Paul's argument. It gives us an infallible explanation of the unbelieving mind or heart. Paul provides a perfect description of the general direction and focus of unbelief in all its manifestations. Thus, this text is indispensable for an understanding of apologetics. If we learn to approach unbelief with the following truths in mind, we will have come a long way in our preparation to give an answer.

ROME WASN'T BUILT . . .

Paul had never visited the church in Rome. He wanted to come and see them (Romans 1:11), but he had not yet had the opportunity. It is not certain how or by whom the church in Rome was founded. We know that it was not founded on one of Paul's missionary journeys. Probably some who heard Peter preach on the Day of Pentecost (Acts 2:10) went back to Rome and started the church there. It could be, then, that the church of Rome was founded even before Paul himself was converted. In any case, Paul wrote to tell them of his desire to visit, and to explain to them the power and glory of the gospel of Jesus Christ.

Paul's explanation of the gospel makes the letter to the Romans stand out among his writings and indeed in the whole

New Testament. Since he had not been there to minister to them personally, he may have wanted to help them understand the gospel that he had been preaching in the course of his missionary journeys. He took it as his apostolic duty to explain the gospel to them. For that reason, the gospel is expressed in this letter in one of the clearest and deepest forms in the entire New Testament.

It may be for that reason that the Lord has seen fit to use the book of Romans in such a marvelous way in the history of the church. Augustine, considered by some to be the greatest of the church fathers, was converted by reading Romans 13:14. Martin Luther, an Augustinian monk, was changed forever by his understanding of Romans 1:17. He was used by God to reform the church and to set some of its most basic principles back in place. Those men who worked for several years to write the Westminster Confession of Faith and Catechisms were more dependent on Augustine than on anyone else. So, behind the greatest church father, the catalyst of the Reformation, and (arguably) the greatest confession of faith ever written, stands the book of Romans. Its truths have been singularly powerful in building up the church of Jesus Christ.

The reason why Paul wrote Romans is implicit in the letter itself. As we read the book, his purpose, or at least one of his purposes, becomes obvious. In order to understand it, we need to think like first-century Christians.

It would be hard to overestimate the radical nature of Christianity in the first century. I remember seeing a documentary about a woman who, in her adult years, found out that she had a living twin somewhere in the world. It was an unsettling discovery. She was excited to know that she had a sibling, but confused to learn that her family was larger than what she had thought all her life. Similarly, the church for centuries had been defined narrowly—by the Lord—as the nation of Israel. But the coming of Christ changed all that, and God's family was suddenly expanded to include Gentiles.

It was not that God's old covenant people were completely cut off. It was rather that others, who had not been included in the old covenant, were now included in God's new covenant people. The dividing wall between the two groups, Jew and Gentile, had been broken down by Jesus Christ (Ephesians 2:14–15). The nation of Israel was no longer the place in which the Lord "housed" his people. They were soon found among many nations—among all nations, eventually. "The people of God" were no longer the nation of Israel, but the church of Jesus Christ, whose members came from every tribe and language and people and nation (Revelation 5:9). This was a radical shift in history. It occurred because God sent his Son Jesus Christ into the world.

It comes as no surprise to us, then, that Christians in the first century struggled to determine their identity. For the most part, they knew that they were not to be identified with the nation of Israel any longer, but just how *should* they be identified? If for centuries God had set his favor on ethnic Israel, how should Gentiles think about themselves and their relationship to God?

Paul wrote to the Roman church to help them with that struggle. There were, it seems, a good number of Jews in the Roman congregation. There were Gentiles as well. It may be that one group was asking about the status of the other. Perhaps accusations were being made. Whatever the case, Paul intended to straighten out the confusion. And he knew that it was in an explanation of the gospel that clarity would come.

Central to the entire book, therefore, is verse 16 of chapter
1. There Paul states why he is "eager to preach the gospel to you
also who are in Rome" (v. 15). He is eager to preach there, he
says in verse 16, because the gospel is "the power of God for salvation to everyone who believes."

That's Paul's first concern—to make sure the Roman Christians understand that this gospel is God's power. It is not just
some notion that Paul has thought up. It is the very power of
God to save. And since the gospel is the power of God, Paul
wants the Romans to know also that he is not ashamed of it.

Why does Paul set the glorious gospel out in terms of
shame? He was probably concerned that the gospel might seem
trivial to some in the shadow of the mighty Roman Empire.
Power in Rome was determined by conquests and wars. It was
symbolized by victories and celebrations. But the gospel is not
like that. It does not define itself by the number of wars won or
victories celebrated. The gospel carries with it the very power
of God. It carries within itself the strength of God himself. As
such, it is able to break down any barrier that might be erected
against God and his people.

> I'm not ashamed to own my Lord,
> Or to defend his cause,
> Maintain the honor of his Word,
> The glory of his cross.
>
> (Isaac Watts)

Paul wants to assure his readers in Rome that this gospel,
of which he is not ashamed, is for the salvation of everyone who
believes, "to the Jew first and also to the Greek" (v. 16). Paul
feels constrained to phrase it this way because of the unity that
the gospel brings.

Now that Jews and Gentiles alike can share in its benefits, one might think that there are no remaining distinctions between the two groups. But that is not the case, either. Paul recognizes in this verse the priority of the Jews in the gospel. God chose them first. The gospel itself came from them, since it originated with Jesus Christ, a Jew (see Matthew 1:1–17). Jesus himself "was sent only to the lost sheep of the house of Israel" (Matthew 15:24). The gospel goes first to Israel, and then to the other nations. That is God's order in history. That is the order the gospel itself has had in the Lord's providence, and Paul wants to recognize that at the outset.

But having said that, there are still serious issues that need to be discussed with respect to the relationship of Jew and Gentile. Paul's concern, particularly in chapters 1 through 11, is to develop that explanation. There is much that needs to be said about our universal condition before God (chaps. 1 and 2), the special place of the Jews, given our universal condition (chap. 3), Abraham's role in all of this (chap. 4), Adam's role (chap. 5), and the relationship of Jew and Gentile in God's electing purposes (chaps. 8–11). These difficult and deeply personal matters were left, in God's providence, to the genius of the apostle Paul to explain—first to the Romans, then to the rest of us. We will focus our attention only on the first chapter of this marvelous letter, and we will attempt to show how useful it is for us as we prepare ourselves for the good fight. Before we do that, however, there are a couple of key concepts that we need to keep in mind.

SHOW AND TELL

One of the most basic truths of the Christian faith is that, in order for us to know God, he must first tell us who he is. This should not surprise us. It is a basic fact of human relationships as well. Human relationships are only as close as the information we choose to give to one another. If I am opening a bank account, for example, the banker will take some basic information from me. He will want to know my full name, address, age, etc. In knowing those things, he will certainly know me, at least to some extent. But the information I give him will be so basic that we would say he doesn't *really* know who I am.

In family relationships, on the other hand, not only is basic information known, but so are patterns of behavior, experiences of joy and pain, likes and dislikes. Typically, we would say that members of our immediate family *really do* know us, and oftentimes know us quite well.

But suppose, as may happen in some cases, a person chooses not to reveal anything about himself. Suppose someone decides that, except for the things that can be discovered easily, he will not share anything about himself, even in his family—not his joys, pains, likes, dislikes, or anything else of a personal nature. It would be quite difficult, even though the person is living in the same house, to get to know that person at all. In order for that person to be known, he would have to be willing to reveal some things about who he is.

If this is the case in family relationships, it is all the more true with God. Because God is not a human being, but rather is completely different from anything created, it is even more true that if we are to get to know him, he must first be willing to tell us who he is.

And God has done that. He has been willing, since the beginning of creation, to tell us who he is, what he likes and dislikes, the things that grieve him and the things that give him delight. The Westminster Confession of Faith addresses this idea:

> The distance between God and the creature is so great,
> that although reasonable creatures do owe obedience
> unto Him as their Creator, yet they could never have
> any fruition of Him as their blessedness and reward,
> but by some voluntary condescension on God's part,
> which He has been pleased to express by way of
> covenant. (7.1)

First, the Confession states that there is a "distance" between God and human beings. This, of course, does not mean that God is physically far away from us (see Acts 17:27). God is not physically anywhere, since he has no physical body. As a matter of fact, God is everywhere (see Psalm 139). What could the Confession mean when it speaks of the "distance" between God and the creature?

The distance spoken of here is really an astounding difference. If we were to think, for example, of the difference between a human being and a fish, we might express that difference by saying that it is impossible for us to "reach" the fish, or for the fish to "reach" us. We are "out of touch" with the ways of the fish. The relationship between God and human beings is like that to some extent. Unlike our relationship with animals, where neither side can really talk to each other, the divide between God and us can be, and has been, bridged by God. God can "reach" us. We can reach him too, if he first reaches us.

This reaching by God is what the Confession calls his "voluntary condescension." God decided that he would "stoop" down to tell us and show us who he is and what he requires of us. He did not have to do that. There was nothing in God, or anything in us, that required him to communicate with us. But, because of his unconditional love for creatures made in his image, he came down to establish a relationship with us. That relationship is often called a "covenant" in Scripture.

God's communication with us takes two forms, and it has taken those forms since the beginning of creation. When God created man as male and female, he gave them certain commands and told them what he required of them:

> And God said to them, "Be fruitful and multiply and fill the earth and subdue it and have dominion over the fish of the sea and over the birds of the heavens and over every living thing that moves on the earth." (Genesis 1:28)

> And the LORD God commanded the man, saying, "You may surely eat of every tree of the garden, but of the tree of the knowledge of good and evil you shall not eat, for in the day that you eat of it you shall surely die." (Genesis 2:16–17)

These commands were given to Adam and Eve. They could not have discovered these instructions by themselves. God came down and told them how to obey him.

This is commonly called God's "special" revelation. What makes it special is that it comes, so to speak, from the very mouth of God. He gives it in verbal form, so that we human beings might know what we otherwise could not discover. It is not special in the sense that it is unique, though it certainly is unique. It is special in the sense that it is specific; it is meant to specify what God wants of us. This kind of revelation most often comes as a "word" from God. It is the kind of revelation that we, the church, now have in the Bible. All of the Bible is God's special revelation to his people.

But there is another kind of revelation. It is often called God's "natural" or "general" revelation. This revelation comes to all people, not just to specific people. It comes to all of creation through the things God has made. This is the revelation that Paul highlights in Romans 1.

Psalm 19 speaks about general revelation. It speaks about it in strong terms:

> The heavens declare the glory of God, and the sky above proclaims his handiwork. Day to day pours out speech, and night to night reveals knowledge. (Psalm 19:1–2)

The psalmist speaks of the heavens *declaring,* of the sky *proclaiming,* of each succeeding day *speaking,* and of each succeeding night *revealing knowledge.* These are terms that we would normally reserve for actual words and speech. But Scripture also connects these terms with what God has created.

So, according to Scripture, God is involved in a "show and tell" presentation. He shows us who he is through the creation. We will discuss this more below, but we should first of all see that God's "showing" is a "proclamation" that gives his human creatures "knowledge." God also tells us who he is, what he thinks, and what he requires, by giving us words. He tells us, ultimately, by giving us his word, the Holy Scriptures.

We will see that this section in Romans is primarily concerned with what God shows in his revelation to all humanity.

Paul first discusses what God has said, of course. He writes first of the righteousness of God as revealed in the gospel. And the gospel is one of those things that God has not revealed in nature.

But he also writes about God showing himself. He writes about God revealing himself in the world, through the world, so that all of us who are made in his image will know the one who made us. In knowing him, we should also serve him. But, as we shall see, because of our sin, that is not our immediate reaction to what God shows us. Our immediate reaction, and our continued action, except for his grace, is to pile sin on sin by trying to repress the very revelation that he gives.

THE GOOD NEWS: REVEALED RIGHTEOUSNESS

Romans 1 gives us both good news and bad news. Both have to do with God's revelation to us. The good news is what God has told us. It is the gospel. It is the gospel of which Paul is not ashamed. *Gospel* means "good news," and the first thing Paul wants his readers to remember is just what that gospel is.

We noted earlier that verse 17 motivated Luther to challenge the doctrine of the Roman church, thus beginning the Reformation. This verse carries with it some of the most important themes of Paul's letter, and it should help us to understand the rest of what he wants to say in chapter 1. We should take a moment, then, to consider it.

Verse 17 continues the thought of verse 16, which we have seen to be the "thesis" verse of Romans. In verse 16, Paul notes that the gospel is the power of God, for Jew and Gentile alike, bringing salvation to all who believe. In verse 17, he tells us that it is the power of God because in it "the righteousness of God is revealed from faith for faith." The power of the gospel is located in the fact that it reveals the righteousness of God. What does Paul mean by this?

One of the most pressing questions in all of humanity is, How can I be accepted by God? It is not that this question is always being asked. We may not actually hear this question very often. But it does lie behind much of our daily activity. So much of what we do is meant to provide significance and meaning to our lives. The only reason to want such things is that we want to be accepted, ultimately, by God himself.

In some ways, we could see all forms of idolatry as an attempt to provide an answer to that question. Whatever else is involved in idolatry (and we will look more closely at that later), part of its appeal is that the gods created by us are also within our grasp and control. It is not difficult to be "accepted" by these gods, since we are the ones who made them.

I well remember an encounter with a Jehovah's Witness who knocked on my door one morning. It was an unusual situation. Normally, they come in pairs, but on this particular morning, he came alone. His name was Lawrence. After listening to what Lawrence wanted to say about his beliefs, I asked him a question. "Given all that you have said," I asked him, "how do you think you can make yourself acceptable to a holy God?" (Lawrence had admitted that he was a sinner.) That question sparked one of the best and most fruitful conversations that I have ever had in that kind of situation.

The question of how we can be accepted by God is one of the most profound questions we can ask. We must have the scriptural answer straight in our minds if we are going to be ready to contend for the faith. It is that question that brought Martin Luther to embrace the gospel for the first time. He knew that he could not be accepted by God, even though he had set his life apart for precisely that purpose! It was this verse in Romans 1, verse 17, that began to soothe his guilty conscience and bring him to an understanding of the liberty of the gospel. This verse, Luther said, "struck my conscience like lightning" and was "like a thunderbolt in my heart."

Paul tells us that the righteousness of God is revealed in the gospel. Another way to say that is to say that the gospel itself is a revelation of God. It tells us something about who God is, as well as what he has done on our behalf. The gospel does not tell us that God has compromised his just and holy character. The gospel does not say that God has ignored his justice for the sake of his grace or his mercy. Rather, it tells us how God can both be just and be gracious to us as well. In that way, it reveals something of the fullness of his character to us.

Perhaps one of the most common misconceptions about God is that he is primarily around to dispense forgiveness to us, no matter what. When I was involved in pastoral ministry, we used to call on people for the purpose of sharing the gospel with them. The vast majority of those with whom we spoke were convinced either that they were forgiven for everything they had done wrong, or that all they needed to do was to ask for forgiveness and they would get it. Forgiveness is what God is there for. It is, we sometimes think, God's "job" to forgive; that's just what he does.

But this understanding of God is far from the true picture that God gives us in his Word. The gospel gives us a true picture of God. It tells us that God is not able to overlook sin because he is holy and just. He can no more ignore or remove these characteristics from himself than he can cease to be good. If he were to do that, he would not be God. He would be a morally weak or compromising person whose standards could be set aside for other goals. This may be the way that we think or act on occasion, but it is not the way God thinks or acts. He cannot set aside his standards; he cannot change his nature. He is bound only by who he himself is. His standards are an expression of who he is, and he is unchangeable.

The gospel tells us that God, rather than overlooking his justice and holiness, sent his Son to pay the penalty that had to be paid if anyone was ever going to be accepted by, and acceptable to, God. It is not that God simply wiped away our penalty. He could not just wipe it off the books and remain a just God. Any human judge who simply winked at the law and let offenders go free would soon lose his position, not to mention his reputation. Even if he did not lose his position, we would be hard-pressed to call him a judge in any meaningful sense of that word.

How much more is this the case with the supreme judge? God cannot simply turn a blind eye to violations of his law. It is a part of his nature that sin must be punished. So God sent his Son to die on the cross to pay the penalty that we deserve. His death on the cross was not his punishment; it was ours. He died for our sins, not his (since he was altogether sinless). As Paul puts it, "For our sake he made him to be sin who knew no sin, so that in him we might become the righteousness of God" (2 Corinthians 5:21).

His Son's sacrifice was acceptable to a holy God, because his Son had lived a perfect life. He had remained holy throughout his life. When he offered himself up as the supreme sacrifice, his sacrifice was acceptable to God since it was a perfect sacrifice. It was offered up by the only perfect high priest. And the only perfect high priest was also the only perfect sacrifice (Hebrews 7:26–8:3). And that, God could accept.

In this way, the righteousness of God is revealed in the gospel. The good news is that God's justice is satisfied; his wrath toward his people has been appeased. Because of what Jesus Christ has done, there is now a way, the only way, to be accepted by a holy God. That way is revealed in the gospel. That way is the way of Jesus Christ. It was only because God made him who had no sin to be sin, that we can become the righteousness of God in him. God's righteousness is revealed in the gospel because the righteousness of God is revealed first in Jesus Christ and then in us through him.

This is why Paul says that the righteousness of God is revealed "from faith for faith." He emphasizes that the righteousness of God, while going out to everyone in the gospel, is not a righteousness that applies to everyone. Remember that the intent of the book of Romans is to explain how the two groups—the Jews and the Gentiles—are brought together under the gospel. This verse gives us a hint. It tells us that Jew and Gentile can share in this revealed righteousness only by faith in Jesus Christ. It tells us, to put it another way, that *anyone* who has faith—"everyone who believes" (v. 16)—is credited with this revealed righteousness as well. The righteousness belongs to Jesus. When we are united to him by faith, we are credited with having righteousness as well. That, in sum, is the good news—the glorious news—that we call the gospel.

This will be Paul's point throughout his letter. The bringing together of Jew and Gentile has taken place in the gospel. And the gospel is, first and foremost, the message that Jesus Christ brings all kinds of people together by faith in him. The priority that Scripture and history give to the Jewish nation is important (see Romans 3:1–2), but it does not bring about preferential treatment from God. Just as "there is no distinction"

between Jew and Gentile, "for *all* have sinned and fall short of
the glory of God," so also "the righteousness of God" comes
"through faith in Jesus Christ for *all* who believe" (Romans
3:22–23).

As Paul's mind is now both on the righteousness of God as
revealed and on the universal extent of the gospel, he begins another line of thinking in verse 18 that will prove to be most significant for apologetics. As is the case with Paul, however, so it
is in apologetics generally, that the gospel must be firmly understood before we can begin to launch into the deep waters of
unbelief. These two key verses, 16 and 17, must therefore be an-
chored in our hearts as we plan, by God's grace, to stand against
the tidal waves of unbelieving thought.

THE BAD NEWS: REVEALED WRATH

As we move from verse 17 to verse 18, there seems at first
glance to be an abrupt change in subject matter. Paul has just
discussed the glorious righteousness of God in the gospel. He
has reminded the Roman Christians that he is in no way
ashamed of, or embarrassed by, that gospel. He knows it is the
power of God. He knows that the gospel, which is focused on
the death and resurrection of Christ (1:2–4), is the very power
and authority of God, breaking down our hard hearts and
bringing us under its liberating control (Romans 6).

But then the topic seems to change significantly. Paul begins to discuss the wrath of God. Is there any connection between the wrath of God and the righteousness of God? There
must be a connection in Paul's mind. This connection is made
more explicit in chapter 2:

> But because of your hard and impenitent heart you are
> storing up wrath for yourself for the day of wrath when
> God's righteous judgment will be revealed. (v. 5)

Or, as Paul says in Romans 11:22:

> Note then the kindness and the severity of God: sever-
> ity toward those who have fallen, but God's kindness to
> you, provided you continue in his kindness. Otherwise
> you too will be cut off.

The revelation of the wrath of God and of his righteousness
come together on the Day of Judgment. What Paul is giving us,
then, in verses 17 and 18, is an understanding of the present connection between God's wrath and his righteousness, a connection that will reach its climax on the day when Christ returns.
But there are at least two other connections in Paul's mind between these two verses.

Verse 18 begins with the word "for," which connects it to
the previous verse. So there is no doubt, simply from the gram-
mar of the passage, that there is a specific connection. Part of
the connection can be seen in the fact that the change in subject
matter is not as radical as it might at first appear. When Paul
discusses righteousness, he shows that this righteousness was
revealed by God. In other words, one of the ideas that Paul de-
velops in this chapter is that God reveals himself in the world
through various means. In the gospel, he reveals his righteousness. Now Paul wants to elaborate on God revealing his wrath.

So Paul is helping us to understand something about God's
revelation in verses 17 and 18, and he is also helping us to understand something about the universality of this revelation. In
verse 16, he tells us that the gospel is for the Jew and the Gen-

tile—two categories that cover the entire human race. The gospel no longer has its focus on the nation of Israel.

Since Christ baptized with the Holy Spirit on the Day of Pentecost, the gospel has had a universal focus. True, it began "in Jerusalem." But it moved to "all Judea and Samaria, and to the end of the earth" (Acts 1:8). There is a universal scope to the gospel, and thus to the revelation of God's righteousness, that is the focus of Paul's attention in these two verses. The gospel is to go out to the whole earth.

In the remainder of this chapter, we will deal only with verse 18. This verse serves as a kind of introduction to a section that continues well into Romans 3. Although we won't look at that entire section, we will want to look at the focus of Paul's argument, especially as it relates to apologetics, in chapter 1 and part of chapter 2. But first, we need to focus on Paul's "introductory" verse. He says:

> For the wrath of God is revealed from heaven against all ungodliness and unrighteousness of men, who by their unrighteousness suppress the truth. (v. 18)

The focus of his concern at this point is the revelation of God's wrath. It may be helpful for us to think for a minute about what the wrath of God is.

The wrath of God is not a popular subject in today's world. It conjures up images of a cruel tyrant imposing penalties on his subjects for the sheer pleasure of exercising his power. That, however, has more to do with caprice than wrath, and is no part of God's character. The dictionary defines *wrath* as "strong, vengeful anger or indignation." That definition comes close to what we mean when we speak of the wrath of God.

It is important to understand that certain of God's characteristics are by-products of who he is in relation to his creation.
Other attributes of God are a part of who he is apart from the
creation. For example, God is triune—Father, Son, and Holy
Spirit. God has always been triune, and he would be whether
or not creation had ever come into existence.

It is not always easy to determine which attribute or char-
acteristic falls into which category. It is sometimes helpful,
though, in thinking about a particular attribute, to ask whether
God could still be God and not have that attribute. If the answer is yes, then it is probably an attribute that *flows from* who
he is.

For example, God is merciful. The Bible speaks of him that
way (see, for example, Psalm 116:5). But his mercy, which is directed toward sinful creatures, is part of his nature only because
of the creation. Before there were creatures, there was no one
to whom God could, or needed to be, merciful. If mercy means
showing favor to someone who does not deserve it, then there
was no one like that around before creation.

God was not merciful prior to creation. He was, however,
love (1 John 4:8, 16). Could God be God and not be love? It
doesn't appear so. Love is an attribute that God shared with
himself, as triune, before there was anything or anyone else.
Love was expressed within the three persons of God. His mercy,
on the other hand, was not expressed between the persons of
the Trinity. There was no need for mercy and no object for its
application. So, God's mercy, rather than being a part of his basic
character, flows from his basic character. It flows from his attribute of love.

God's wrath is like his mercy. It is an attribute that was neither needed nor present before the creation of the world. What,

then, is God's wrath? At its root, it is an aspect of God's character that flows from his holiness. Remember that holiness refers, first of all, to God's "difference." Remember, too, that we often use spatial terms to communicate this difference. We talk of God as being "above" us, or "beyond" his creation. We think of him sometimes as "outside" of space and time. All of these terms give us a picture of what we mean by holiness.

The Bible itself uses this kind of terminology (see, for example, Psalm 108:5). But we also know from Scripture that God is not really distant from his creation; he is in and with it, since he is everywhere (Psalm 139:7–14). The idea of God's holiness is meant to express this fundamental difference in God. He is essentially different from everything else.

But it is also meant to express God's "distance" from everything that is unholy. When we speak of God as holy, we are saying that he is both separated from, and vengeful toward, sin. Sin is a violation of God's law. That law is an expression of his character. It is holy, righteous, and good (Romans 7:12). When God's law is violated, there is a violation, not simply of some rule or regulation, as with our laws, but of his character as God. The fact that God is holy means that he must punish all such violations. Because of who he is, he cannot sit idly by while his character is attacked.

That, in its simplest form, is what the wrath of God is. It is the expression of his holiness toward sin. It is his just and righteous reaction to transgressions of his law, and thus of his character. When the Bible speaks of the wrath of God, it is speaking of his response to man's response to his law.

This should help us understand something about the wrath of God that will be important in the next chapter. God's wrath is not a random, capricious act that he exercises on a whim.

God does not do anything arbitrarily. Everything he does is for a perfect reason, and it is done with perfect timing and perfect effect.

The revelation of his wrath is perfect as well. It is God's answer to a response that we have already chosen. His wrath is an expression of his attitude toward our sinful choices. In that way, it is like a parent's punishment of a child. It would be sinful and wrong for a parent to punish his child simply because he felt like lashing out at somebody. True punishment is a response to a child's wrong choice. It is meant to provide correction and good direction. But it would not come in the first place if the child obeyed the parent's rules.

So the wrath of God, revealed from heaven, is a response on his part. It is directed "against all ungodliness and unrighteousness of men, who by their unrighteousness suppress the truth."

God's wrath takes on a form that we may not expect. We will look at that form in the next chapter. We will look, as well, at the reason that God's wrath comes. That reason will have important significance for our apologetic endeavors.

DIGGING DEEPER

1. How can we demonstrate that we are not ashamed of the gospel?
2. How is God manifested in creation?
3. How do God's justice and holiness relate to his wrath?
4. How would you describe God's wrath to an unbeliever?
5. Does the unbeliever have any kind of relationship with God? How would you describe that relationship?

5

THE DIVINE PSYCHOLOGIST

As we saw in the last chapter, Paul begins this glorious letter to the Romans by reminding us of the good news of the gospel and also introducing us to the reality of God's wrath. As we will see in this chapter, the wrath of God is his response to our wicked response to him. In outlining the sinful response that we all give to God, Paul introduces us to divine psychology.

Science is typically divided into two categories—hard sciences and soft sciences. Hard science, such as physics and chemistry, tends to use specific rules, laws, and procedures to carry on its work. The laws of physics can be depended on and used in making observations and calculations. They are "hard" facts.

Soft sciences, on the other hand, are not as predictable. Because of their subject matter, they have to be more tentative about their conclusions. In many of the soft sciences, such as psychology and sociology, the subject matter is human beings. Because of their complexity, these sciences have to be careful to avoid applying their conclusions too broadly. While physics can

> For what can be known about God is plain to them, because God has shown it to them. For his invisible attributes, namely, his eternal power and divine nature, have been clearly perceived, ever since the creation of the world, in the things that have been made. So they are without excuse. For although they knew God, they did not honor him as God or give thanks to him, but they became futile in their thinking, and their foolish hearts were darkened. Claiming to be wise, they became fools, and exchanged the glory of the immortal God for images resembling mortal man and birds and animals and reptiles.
>
> Therefore God gave them up in the lusts of their hearts to impurity, to the dishonoring of their bodies among themselves, because they exchanged the truth about God for a lie and worshiped and served the creature rather than the Creator, who is blessed forever! Amen.

speak confidently about the properties of energy wherever it may be found, psychology does not have that luxury. In a soft science, it is more difficult to set up, and to count on, hard and fast laws that can be easily reproduced.

Partly because it is a soft science, the practice of psychology can be quite diverse. With over 250 schools of psychology in the United States today, it is difficult to find a common thread that ties them together. But if we examine the meaning of the word *psychology* itself, perhaps we can understand its basic meaning.

The Greek word *psychē* means (something like) "soul." The suffix "ology" comes from a Greek word meaning "word" or "topic" or "study." So *psychology* means (something like) "the study of the soul." This is one of the reasons why psychology is not a hard science. It is a soft science because human behavior is so unpredictable.

*For this reason God gave them up to dishonorable passions.
For their women exchanged natural relations for those that are
contrary to nature; and the men likewise gave up natural relations with women and were consumed with passion for one another, men committing shameless acts with men and receiving in
themselves the due penalty for their error.*

*And since they did not see fit to acknowledge God, God gave
them up to a debased mind to do what ought not to be done. They
were filled with all manner of unrighteousness, evil, covetousness,
malice. They are full of envy, murder, strife, deceit, maliciousness.
They are gossips, slanderers, haters of God, insolent, haughty,
boastful, inventors of evil, disobedient to parents, foolish, faithless,
heartless, ruthless. Though they know God's decree that those who
practice such things deserve to die, they not only do them but give
approval to those who practice them. —Romans 1:19–32*

To God, however, psychology (like all other sciences) is a
hard science (so to speak). Whatever the mysteries and conun-
drums surrounding the human psyche may be, God knows
them all, at all times, completely and exhaustively. Divine psychology, therefore, is infallible and comprehensive. When God
gives a diagnosis, it is beyond dispute. He knows the end from
the beginning, and everything in between, without error and
without doubt. When God speaks about the human psyche,
therefore, we would be wise to listen carefully.

In Romans 1:18–32, it is the activity of the human soul, what
we might simply call the "inner person," that God is describing for us. He gives us the kind of information that we could
never have access to by ourselves. We have no infallible analysis of the human condition; we have no way of getting inside
every person to see what is going on there. But God does. And

when he does tell us, in his Word, what is going on in the "inner recesses" of a person, we should not simply believe it, but apply those truths. It just so happens that God's evaluation of the human psyche in Romans 1 is immensely helpful for defending and commending the Christian faith.

KNOWING GOD

It is often difficult to follow the train of thought in a biblical passage. Sometimes, just when you think you understand a particular argument in Scripture, the next verse challenges everything you thought you knew about the passage. I well remember beginning to work on a sermon and thinking that the passage that I had selected was fairly straightforward. The more deeply I looked into that passage, however, the more I realized how little I understood of what the writer (Paul) was actually trying to say. My only comfort was that the apostle Peter himself admitted that there were things in Paul that were difficult to understand (2 Peter 3:15–16). If Peter had trouble understanding some things in Scripture, then surely we will too.

In the passage that we will be looking at in this chapter, however, this problem is not as serious. Although no one would claim exhaustive knowledge of what Paul is arguing here, this section in Romans is one of those rare places where you can almost see Paul's brilliant mind at work as he writes. It should help us, then, to follow his line of thinking.

Paul's initial concern in this section is to show that all of us are in the same condition with respect to our relationship to God. He highlights the universal character of sin as it applies to and affects each and every one of us.

Paul has just explained that the gospel now has a universal dimension that was not present under the old covenant. The gospel may be for Jews first, but it is for Gentiles as well. It is to go out to the ends of the earth. The question then arises, What is the state of those to whom the gospel goes? Am I taking the gospel to people who are otherwise innocent, given that they have not heard the gospel? When the gospel goes out to the heathen, will they have any idea of who this God is that we talk about?

Paul weaves together two basic ideas in this passage. First, he wants us to understand the response of those who are outside of Christ to the knowledge of God. Second, he tells us about God's response to that (sinful) response. We will see how these two ideas fit together.

We saw in the last chapter that God reveals both the gospel and his wrath. Paul focuses on the wrath of God in the rest of Romans 1. He is concerned to tell us why this wrath comes. He wants us to see why and in what circumstances God responds in wrath, rather than in grace or in mercy.

So he begins, in verse 18, by telling us that God's wrath is revealed from heaven, and that it is directed against the wickedness of men. This does not mean that God reveals his wrath only where wickedness is the worst. The revelation of God's wrath is universal, and it comes against "all ungodliness and unrighteousness of men." God's wrath is revealed everywhere, manifesting his anger at the universal wickedness of sinful human beings.

Paul then introduces an idea that he knows will require more explanation. He describes these godless and wicked people as those "who by their unrighteousness suppress the truth." This could also be translated as "who hold down the truth in unrighteousness." The explanation of this idea will occupy Paul's thinking for much of chapter 1 and some of chapter 2.

This notion that sinners suppress the truth will need some clarification, and Paul knows that. The first question that comes to mind is, What truth? Paul anticipates that question and begins to answer it in verse 19. The truth that is suppressed is "what can be known about God." And what that is, Paul says, is "plain to them." The word translated as "plain" could just as easily be translated as "clear" or "evident." Whatever it is that is known about God is something that is clear. It is not something that only a few can see, or that is otherwise hidden or obscure. "What can be known about God" is as plain and clear as the world around us.

But it is clear, not because we see so well, or because we have used our minds to discover it, but "because God has shown it to them." This is a significant truth that deserves a good deal of thought. What we learn here is that there is a knowledge of God that is plain and clear, precisely because God has made it plain and clear. Paul is directing us here to the revealing activity of God.

As we saw in the last chapter, this kind of revelation from God is commonly referred to as God's "general revelation." Both words are important to understand. It is *general* revelation because it goes out to all people. A standard dictionary definition of the word *general* is this: "involving, relating to, or applicable to every member of a class, kind, or group." This is the way the word is used here. Paul is describing a revelation that involves, relates to, and is applicable to every person. He is not thinking here of *special* revelation, which is intended for God's special people, the church of Jesus Christ. But this revelation is universal. For that reason, it is general.

It is important to notice here what Paul does *not* have in mind. General revelation is not a revelation that can save us. The gospel is not part of its content (see Romans 10:7–15). General revelation does not contain what is needed for a saving knowledge of God.

This is obvious from the context. Paul begins with a revelation of God's wrath, not of his grace. He reminds us that God's wrath is revealed against those who are wicked and godless. Their wickedness and godlessness are bound up with their suppression of the truth. Paul is explaining to us what truth is suppressed in wickedness.

We now know that it is truth about God, truth that God himself makes plain, and which, therefore, is plain to all of us. We should emphasize here that Paul is discussing *God's* activity, not ours. He is affirming that we do, in fact, plainly see, and therefore know, God. But this knowledge has not come about as a result of our intellectual efforts, any more than it has come about because we have been looking for God. There is no one who seeks God (Romans 3:11). "What can be known about God" is known because it is *given by God,* not because of any encouragement that we have received, or effort that we have expended, to know or see him. God is the one acting here; we are passive receptacles of this revelation of himself.

But Paul does not tell us specifically what he means by "what may be known about God." Again, he anticipates the question that his readers might have: What is it that may be known about God? Paul answers that question in the next verse.

In order to answer that question, Paul takes us all the way back to the creation of the world. This is one of the reasons that we can tell that Paul is thinking universally at this point. He is not thinking about isolated individuals or groups. Rather, he is pointing us to the beginning of this revelation, this plain and clear manifestation that God gives. He tells us that this general revelation has been given by God to us "ever since the creation of the world" (v. 20).

This reference to creation tells us that God's general revelation is not itself a response to sin. It is not as though God decided after Adam's sin that he should make himself known in a different way than he had done before the Fall. God's general revelation is embedded in creation itself. From the time that God created man and woman in his image, he has revealed himself through his creation—plainly *to* us and *in* us.

God has revealed in creation his "invisible attributes, namely, his eternal power and divine nature" (v. 20). Charles Hodge is probably correct in his commentary on this passage. He notes that these terms are comprehensive in scope. "Eternal power and divine nature" are not specific attributes or perfections of God. Rather, says Hodge, this general revelation of God to all men includes "all the divine perfections."[1] The general terms include the more specific terms.

The Westminster Confession of Faith has as good a summary of these perfections as can be found:

> There is but one only, living, and true God, who is infinite in being and perfection, a most pure spirit, invisible, without body, parts, or passions; immutable, immense, eternal, incomprehensible, almighty, most wise,

1. Charles Hodge, *Commentary on the Epistle to the Romans* (reprint, Grand Rapids: Eerdmans, 1980), 37. While it may not be the case that every person knows every attribute of God at every point, Paul's point in using the general categories of "eternal power" and "divine nature" is to include all of those specific attributes of God that make him God. So, in verse 32, we see that even unbelievers know that their disobedience is worthy of death. This knowledge requires a prior knowledge of, for example, God's holiness and justice.

most holy, most free, most absolute; working all things according to the counsel of His own immutable and most righteous will, for His own glory; most loving, gracious, merciful, long-suffering, abundant in goodness and truth, forgiving iniquity, transgression, and sin; the rewarder of them that diligently seek Him; and withal, most just, and terrible in His judgments, hating all sin, and who will by no means clear the guilty. (2.1)

All of this, says Paul, *is made known* by God and *is known* by all of humanity. This, obviously, is not just a vague and imprecise knowledge; it is not a capacity for knowledge or a potential knowledge that needs supplementation. Neither is it simply a feeling or an abstract idea. Paul is not saying that we all have some idea that there is *a* god *somewhere*.

This is true, certain, clear, and rich knowledge of *God himself*. Paul makes this even clearer in verse 19, where he speaks of "what can be known about God." This could be better translated as "knowing God." This is the truth of the matter: All of us, all creatures made in the image of God, *know God!* Paul could not be clearer here. His language is straightforward and unambiguous. Even those who are outside of Christ, because they live and move in God's creation, because God makes himself plain in that creation, clearly and plainly know him.

Just to make sure he gets his point across, Paul says again in verse 20 that this revelation that God gives has been "clearly perceived, ever since the creation of the world, in the things that have been made." God, who created us, leaves no room for ignorance in his human creatures.

We should remember where Paul began this discussion. He began with the revelation of God's wrath. He spelled out for us that God's wrath is against our wickedness. He then let us know that at the root of our wicked hearts lies, not ignorance, but a suppression of the truth. That suppression frames our wickedness; it is the defining element of it. Now we learn that the truth that is suppressed is actually the clear and universal knowledge of God, which is given by God himself.

We should not pass over lightly the weight of Paul's analysis of unbelief here. He is telling us that there are no true atheists. To be sure, someone will say in his heart (as the psalmist reminds us), "There is no God" (Psalm 14:1). But the psalmist calls him a fool, at least in part because he says in his heart what is obviously not the case. This is the height of folly. The fool says in his heart what he knows is not the case. Atheism, we can now say, taking into account what Paul has taught us, is simply a suppression of the true knowledge of God.

The way that Paul expresses this truth requires us to say, without hesitation, that all people know God. This does not mean that all people believe *that* there is a god. We are not saying that the knowledge that people have is like an empty belief—a belief in UFOs, for example. I may believe *that* there are UFOs, but I have no evidence for that belief and it (hopefully) will have little effect on my everyday life. Paul is *not* saying that the knowledge of God that all people have is like that. It is not a knowledge without evidence, a knowledge that has no effect on our living. As a matter of fact, it is exactly the opposite.

This knowledge that all human beings have is knowledge of a *person*. It is God whom all people know. This means that all people are in a relationship with God. To be sure, the wicked are not, and cannot be (apart from Christ), in a saving relationship with God. But they are in a relationship nevertheless. Perhaps the wicked can be compared to someone who is in prison. What relationship does a person in prison have to his government? He is certainly not "out of a relationship" with his government. He knows his government all too well, as he lives in the environment that it provides. As a matter of fact, he is where he is, and his life is the way it is, because of his response to his government's laws. He remains in a relationship to his government, though not a happy one.

The same is true of those wicked and godless men who suppress the truth in unrighteousness. Since Paul is describing unbelief generally here, we could say that the same is true of all those who are outside of Christ. We are related to God in that we know him. We know what he is like; we are confronted with him day by day as we live and move and exist in him (Acts 17:28).

This could be called a covenantal relationship. A covenant is a contractual relationship between two or more people. This relationship is initiated by God himself. He has been revealing himself since the creation of the world. Our obligation is to acknowledge this revelation and to repent (Romans 2:4). These are the terms of the contract. Instead of repenting, however, we hold down the truth that comes through this revelation. So we are contract, or covenant, breakers. But being a covenant breaker assumes that there was a covenant there in the first place. Since we know God, and refuse to repent of our wickedness, preferring to hold down that knowledge, we are still relating to him as we live in this world.

There is one further point, a most important point, that Paul makes in verse 20. Since all people know God, and since this knowledge has come by the clear, ongoing revelation of God in the world, Paul concludes that those who suppress that knowledge are "without excuse." The Greek word translated as "without excuse" is used in the New Testament only here and in Romans 2:1. It is transliterated into English as *anapologētos*. It is related to the Greek word for "apologetics," and could easily be translated as "without an apologetic." Those who suppress the knowledge of God that he continues to give them through his creation, are now, as they will be on the Day of Judgment, *without a defense* before God.

This is good news for Christians as we continue to prepare ourselves to do apologetics. We are aware of the fact that people have devised elaborate philosophies and theories in order to avoid the clear knowledge of God that is both within them and evident around them. We know that opposition to God is not silenced. But, Paul tells us here, all of these philosophies, all of these theories, all of the objections lodged against the knowledge of God, amount to nothing in the end. All opposing positions are ultimately indefensible.

Again, we need to train our minds to think this way. We need to believe God rather than man. No matter how intimidating, or how articulate, or how sophisticated they may be, the arguments raised up against Christianity are not capable of a reasoned defense. This must be burned in our hearts: *Any and every position that is opposed to Christianity is utterly indefensible.*

Of course, when we step back and think about it, we know this to be the case, if we are Christians. We know that Christianity, and Christianity alone, is true. We know this by the grace of God, not by our own wisdom. But we do know it. Any position, therefore, that stands opposed to Christianity is necessarily false. And a false position is false, in part, because it is unable to deal with the way things really and truly are. A false position or statement attempts to say something about the world that is simply not true or real.

So those who suppress the knowledge of God in unrighteousness are in the business of constantly denying what is real, what is true. The world they see with sinful eyes is not the real world. It is not the world where God reigns in Christ. It is not the world where our purpose is to glorify him and enjoy him forever. It is a false world, where something reigns besides God and where we are meant to glorify our own desires and wishes. But this world is not the real world. How then could it possibly be defended? Paul reminds us that it cannot. Those who suppress the truth are without a defense—they have no apologetic.

It is important to realize, as well, what Paul is telling us about evidences for God's existence. Much ink has been spilled on the question of evidences for God's existence. Paul is saying in these verses that everything is evidence for God's existence. The argument is simple and straightforward. The poet Joseph Addison understood this:

> The spacious firmament on high,
> With all the blue ethereal sky,
> And spangled heav'ns, a shining frame,
> Their great Original proclaim.
> Th' unwearied sun, from day to day,
> Does his Creator's pow'r display,
> And publishes to ev'ry land
> The work of an almighty hand.
>
> Soon as the evening shades prevail,
> The moon takes up the wondrous tale,
> And nightly to the list'ning earth
> Repeats the story of her birth;
> Whilst all the stars that round her burn,
> And all the planets in their turn,

Confirm the tidings as they roll,
And spread the truth from pole to pole.

What though in solemn silence all
Move round this dark terrestrial ball?
What though no real voice nor sound
Amidst their radiant orbs be found?
In reason's ear they all rejoice,
And utter forth a glorious voice;
Forever singing, as they shine,
"The hand that made us is divine."

God is known through the things that are made. Everything, except God, has been made. Therefore, God is known through everything.

Evidence for God's existence is abundant; there is no place in the entirety of the universe that does not evidence his existence. In that sense, everything proves God. It does not do so in the same way that an argument proves God. But everything proves God nevertheless because it "shouts" of his existence and attributes.

There is a passage in the Old Testament that relates to Paul's teaching here. In Psalm 19, David says:

The heavens declare the glory of God, and the sky above proclaims his handiwork. Day to day pours out speech, and night to night reveals knowledge. (vv. 1–2)

As we noted earlier, David is speaking of creation, but he is using verbs that are normally associated with words and statements. The heavens *declare,* the sky *proclaims,* the successive days pour out *speech,* and the successive nights reveal *knowledge.*

David uses this "language" terminology to describe natural revelation. God's revelation in nature is something that declares and proclaims; it pours out speech and reveals knowledge. The evidence for God's existence is far from lacking; it reveals God clearly, visibly, understandably, and universally in each and every thing that is made, from the smallest particle to the greatest galaxy.

I remember talking with a man whose job was to operate an electron microscope. This microscope was designed to magnify things that were invisible to the naked eye and to any other kind of microscope. He asked some colleagues to bring him some man-made things that were, to our eyes, smooth, fine, and sharp. One person brought in a razor blade. He placed that blade in the microscope. This smooth, sharp razor was, when magnified in the microscope, filled with holes, irregularities, grooves, and flaws.

He then placed some small living organisms in that microscope. They were seen to contain amazing intricacies and complexities that were invisible to the naked eye—and no flaws. Surely, no human could make such a thing. Our finest "creations" are flawed and ugly, even when compared to the smallest things of God's creation.

Comparing the finest things that man can make to the things of nature gives abundant evidence that the best that man can do is almost infinitely worse than the smallest molecules and atoms that God has created. This is clear and plain evidence of the Creator. There is no lack of evidence for God's existence.

A story is told about the English philosopher Bertrand Russell. Russell was no friend of Christianity. One of his most famous lectures was entitled "Why I Am Not a Christian." Someone once asked Russell to consider what would happen if he were wrong. "What would happen," Russell was asked, "if you die and immediately find yourself before God? What will you say?" Russell responded, "I will say to him, 'Not enough evidence! Not enough evidence!'"

If Paul is right (and he is), it is certain that Russell did not respond that way when he died. There is abundant evidence for God's existence. Russell spent his whole life and career refusing to see or believe what was clearly revealed to him. Instead of accepting the obvious, he concocted a number of theories and arguments to show either that God did not exist, or, if he did exist, that his existence did not impinge upon everyday life. Many were under the impression that Russell's arguments against Christianity were sound, but they were not. He was without an apologetic.

When he died, Russell found himself before his Creator and Judge. Whatever his plea, he could not say to God that there was not enough evidence. He could not even plead ignorance. Russell knew God. He knew God because he was God's creature, made in his image. He knew God because he lived, moved, and had his being in him (Acts 17:28).

Paul says that the evidence for God's existence is everywhere and in everything. Even those who never open their eyes have evidence of God's existence because they themselves are that evidence. Not only is the evidence abundant, but because it is revealed to us by God, it is clear, and clearly seen, as well as understood. But it is suppressed. Paul goes on to tell us what that suppression looks like.

AN IDOL FACTORY

John Calvin once remarked that the human heart is a *fab-ricum idolarum,* an idol factory. Paul is about to give us one of the main reasons why people are perpetually serving false gods. Idolatry is the expression of the suppression of the knowledge of God within us. In verse 19, we find that the suppression of the truth in unrighteousness manifests itself in ingratitude. Those who know God, but refuse to acknowledge him, do not honor him; they do not give thanks.

It is perhaps a routine thing for those who know Christ to thank the Lord for their food each time they sit down to eat. Why go through such repetition? Why not just acknowledge that God made all things and gives us good gifts and be through with it? The answer to that, in part, is that our being sanctified in Christ includes the ongoing gratitude that we have for what God has done for and in us. Ingratitude is similar to pride. If we are ungrateful for what we have, then we presume to have gotten it merely by our own efforts. That is an affront to the gracious and good character of the God who supplies good things to and for us all.

As we saw, it is the fool who says in his heart that there is no God. Those who remain outside of Christ, as they suppress the knowledge of God, express that suppression by failing to give thanks (v. 21). It has been said that the essence of the Christian life is gratitude. As sinners saved by grace, we should be constantly thankful for the relationship we have to God and for his grace (1 Thessalonians 5:18). If that is the case, we could also say that ingratitude typically marks the attitude of those who are outside of Christ. This ingratitude might express itself as an insistence that we have whatever we have because we worked hard and earned it. We have it because we deserve to have it. We have it because we did it ourselves.

So, says Paul, this ingratitude turns into a boastful pride. Those who refuse to acknowledge God profess to be wise (v. 22). They count themselves among the intellectual elite. Not only do they refuse to give thanks, but because they think they have earned what they have, they also think that they must be pretty intelligent. One deceptive turn deserves another. There is a move from thinking we deserve what we have, to convincing ourselves that we got it because of our abilities.

The word *philosophy* is a combination of two Greek words that mean "love of wisdom." Philosophers are those who claim to love knowledge for the sake of knowledge alone, as the Greek philosopher Aristotle once said. They ask big questions—Who am I? What is the nature of the universe? How can I know anything? What is right and wrong?—and then they formulate answers to those questions. Unfortunately, in the long history of philosophy, the answers given to those big questions have turned out to be, for the most part, foolish. Paul may have had this in mind as he wrote. Those who profess to have wisdom often turn out to be the most foolish. A quick read of most any textbook in philosophy will prove Paul's point.

But it is *how* this foolishness arises that is of interest to us. It is not because they profess to be wise that they are fools. Professing wisdom may be boastful, but it does not automatically make one foolish. No, Paul says that foolishness comes about because of an exchange.

We sometimes speak of "the great exchange" of the gospel: Christ became what he was not, so that we might become what we are not. He became sin, so that we might become righteous in him. This is the glory of the gospel.

The exchange that Paul speaks about here is not glorious or great, but grotesque. It is the quintessential perversion. Those who suppress the truth in unrighteousness "exchanged the glory of the immortal God for images" (v. 23). Suppression of the truth reveals itself as idolatry.

Paul elaborates on this point in verse 25: "They exchanged the truth about God for a lie and worshiped and served the creature rather than the Creator." This exchange begins by setting aside what should come naturally to us. We are made in God's image. As people made in God's image, we were created to glorify him in worship and service. That is our "natural" condition because we were made that way.

This suppression of the truth, however, does not set aside all worship and service. It attempts to take God out of the picture and put some created thing in his place. In our wickedness, we exchange the one we ought to worship for something else that we would rather worship.

This tells us a great deal about those who continue to walk in unbelief. They are not able, as God's creatures, simply to cease worshiping and serving. Since they refuse to worship and serve the true God, who constantly reveals himself to them, they must substitute something else in his place.

Think about your own worship of God and your service of him, if you are in Christ. Suppose someone comes to you and orders you to give it up. What would you say? Like many in the early church and even to the present day, you would probably say that you could not, that you must obey God rather than men (Acts 5:29). The worship of God is necessary for a Christian. It is an essential part of who we are in Christ. If we are commanded to give it up, we simply cannot obey that command. We will hold on to it with our very lives.

Now transfer that kind of allegiance to someone who is outside of Christ, who worships and serves an idol. What will he think if you come to him and tell him, as we do in apologetics and in the preaching of the gospel, that he must give up his worship and service of that created thing? He may react as those in Christ would react. He may want to hold on to it for dear life. He may think that he would rather die than give it up.

Such is the nature of idolatry. It is not simply a casual or accidental allegiance to something else. Those who worship the sun do not do so casually or because they are trying to fill their time. They hold steadfastly to their objects of worship. This may be one of the reasons why we seem to have so many "addictions" around today. We may have lost the vocabulary to call these things what Paul calls them. They are idols, and idols are made to be worshiped and served with everything in us. They can hold us in their grasp and instill in us more and more wickedness.

This is what the suppression of the truth looks like. It worships, but it does not worship God. It serves, but it denies God what is due him and so serves an idol. It values wisdom, but is actually foolish. It claims to have truth, but is actually a lie. This leads to a mass of sinful confusion in the lives of unbelievers.

We know, however, where this confusion comes from. It comes from the suppressed knowledge of God. It comes from the exchange that produces idolatry and more wickedness in the hearts of its supporters.

GETTING WHAT WE WANT

Up to this point, Paul has been explaining what he meant in verse 18 when he wrote of the suppression of truth. He de-velops that idea, roughly, up to verse 24. Beginning at verse 24, he begins to explain what the wrath of God looks like as it is revealed from heaven. What it looks like is given to us in some graphic detail.

Suppression of the truth leads to a grotesque exchange. It leads to behavior that is opposed to God and to his service. But it also leads to something that God does, rather than something that we do. Notice this phrase in verses 24, 26, and 28: "God gave them up." What could Paul mean by that?

There is no question in Scripture that God is good to his entire creation (Psalm 145:9). He bestows good gifts on all of his creatures. He causes the rain and the sunshine to fall on both the just and the unjust (Matthew 5:44–45). He blessed the Egyptians for the sake of Joseph (Genesis 39:5). He gives people good things in this life, even to those who will be condemned (Luke 16:25). This should not be taken lightly by those of us who are in Christ. God knows who is condemned; he knows who will refuse to trust him. Yet he still gives them good things and provides for them, even in the midst of their rebellion.

God also restrains his wrath (Genesis 6:3). He does not judge wickedness immediately (Psalm 50:21). Even as he restrains his wrath, he restrains sin (Genesis 20:6). Although people are sinful through and through, that sinfulness does not come to its full expression because, and only because, God restrains the wicked from carrying out their evil desires.

But Paul is telling us here in Romans that there will be situations in which God will lift those restraints. As we read in Genesis 6:3, God's Spirit will not strive with men forever. There will come a time when some of those who refuse to acknowledge God will be "given up" by God to live out the wickedness that they have chosen for themselves. This "giving up" is an ex-

pression of the wrath of God. So when we see these circumstances, we should see them as examples of the wrath of God
being revealed in and through these sins.

Paul's examples of wrath focus, in the first place, on those
acts which are supremely unnatural. This is what we might expect in a passage that tells us about God's revelation in nature.
We can recognize God's wrath when we see rebellion and perversion of the natural order of things.

When God lifts his gracious restraints on people who refuse to acknowledge the revelation of his character in nature,
these people will begin to pervert and distort the very nature
that reveals God in the first place. They will do this in an attempt to further suppress the truth. If they could (though it is
quite impossible) blot the natural out completely, then they
would be done with the revelation of God in it. In an attempt
to destroy that revelation in nature, they distort the natural to
the point where they hope it will be unrecognizable. If it is unrecognizable, then God will not be seen so clearly in it.

When God's merciful restraints on sin are lifted in some,
men and women will take what is meant to be a good and natural blessing, sexual relations in the context of marriage, and
not simply ignore the limits by refusing to marry, but completely
distort the blessing itself by changing it into something that it
was never created to be. The beauty of the relationship between
Adam and Eve (Genesis 2:23) becomes the ugliness of self-
centered distortion.

Paul's list of sins that begins in verse 29 consists of sins that
we are all familiar with. The interesting thing is that this list is
a description of the revelation of God's wrath! These sins are
violations of the law of God, but they are also evidence of the
fact that God is angry with the responses he receives from those

who take his good gifts, who know him because he reveals himself to them, yet who steadfastly refuse to honor him, give him thanks, or acknowledge him as God.

So, there is evidence of God even in the wicked and sinful things that we see around us. Those sins, as evidence of the corruption of the person, are also evidence of God's anger toward sin and the removal of his gracious restraint of sin in the lives of some who rebel.

MISERY LOVES COMPANY

There is one more matter that we should note in the last verse of Romans 1. In verse 32, Paul sums up his discussion by explaining to us that those who know God and yet suppress the truth, know something else. In knowing God, because of his revelation in creation, they also know his righteous "decree." That is, they know what God requires of them.

Paul will elaborate on what he means by this in the next chapter. The important point for us, however, is that, along with this revelation that God gives of himself, he gives his requirements and penalties. Put simply, he gives his law (Romans 2:14–16). Along with knowing the requirements of God's law, the wicked also know that those who disobey his law "deserve to die."

But what is the response of the wicked who know that they deserve to die for their evil deeds? Paul says that "they not only do them but give approval to those who practice them." A rational response would be to avoid those things that cause our destruction. But sin is not rational. It does not respond to things in a way that seems obvious. Instead of trying to avoid destructive behavior, the wicked gather together in groups. They become activists and picket and petition for their own wicked causes. They focus on their personal rights, and attempt to make everyone else do the same.

If we need a map to help us understand our culture, Romans 1 is a good place to begin. It is essential that we look there if we are going to be biblical in our defense of the faith. It will make a world of difference if we can trust what the apostle Paul says about unbelief, even before we take the unbeliever at his word.

If we understand that all people know the God of whom we speak, if we know that they know the truth, then we will never feel as though the truth that we defend, and that we communicate to them, is irrelevant. They may act as though it is irrelevant. They may act as though they have no interest at all in the discussion. But Paul tells us that that is exactly what they are doing—acting. They are putting on a false face in an effort to destroy the truth that they know and that you are communicating to them in your apologetic.

Divine psychology is infallible. It describes exactly what goes on in the human mind. When that psychology is applied to the unbelieving mind, our only option is to trust it completely. All people know God—that is the truth of the matter. When we defend the faith, we speak to people who are not ignorant of our God. Our apologetics must take that into account when we are called upon to defend the faith.

> Blind unbelief is sure to err,
> And scan his work in vain;
> God is his own interpreter,
> And he will make it plain.
>   (William Cowper)

Of course, what God makes plain is suppressed. Blind unbelief is sure to err just because it is blind. The knowledge of God is suppressed to such an extent that unbelievers, in and of themselves, will not acknowledge that they know him. That will make the matter complicated at times. But they do know him, and our defense attempts to bring out that which they know to be true, in order to show them how the gospel is the only remedy for their "grotesque exchange." Our hope and prayer is that they will worship and serve the Creator, "who is blessed forever! Amen" (Romans 1:25).

DIGGING DEEPER

1. How can you tell if someone is suppressing the truth in unrighteousness?
2. What difference does it make that the knowledge of God gained through creation is knowledge of a *person,* not simply of facts?
3. Why does Paul include worship in his description of the unbeliever's exchange? What characteristics of worship would an unbeliever exhibit?
4. Where do you see evidence of God's restraint of sin in society?
5. How does Paul's description of the unbelieving heart help you in your approach to apologetics?

6

JERUSALEM MEETS ATHENS: APOLOGETICS IN ACTION

F. F. Bruce has said that Acts 17 "is one of the earliest examples of Christian apologetic against the pagans, designed to show that the true knowledge of God is given in the gospel and not in the idolatrous vanities of paganism."[1] The narrative of Paul's meeting at the Areopagus provides a good example of biblical apologetics.

Paul was on his second missionary journey. Jews in Thessalonica had stirred up opposition to Paul there, so he and Silas and Timothy went fifty miles south to Berea. Unfortunately, some Jews followed them to Berea to stir up opposition to Paul there also. So some Christian brothers took Paul to Athens, leaving Silas and Timothy behind. Paul sent the brothers back with a request for Silas and Timothy to join him in Athens as soon as they could (Acts 17:13–15).

1. F. F. Bruce, *The Book of the Acts,* The New International Commentary on the New Testament (Grand Rapids: Eerdmans, 1986), 24.

Those who conducted Paul brought him as far as Athens, and
after receiving a command for Silas and Timothy to come to
him as soon as possible, they departed.

Now while Paul was waiting for them at Athens, his spirit
was provoked within him as he saw that the city was full of
idols. So he reasoned in the synagogue with the Jews and the
devout persons, and in the marketplace every day with those
who happened to be there. Some of the Epicurean and Stoic
philosophers also conversed with him. And some said, "What
does this babbler wish to say?" Others said, "He seems to be a
preacher of foreign divinities"—because he was preaching
Jesus and the resurrection. And they took hold of him and
brought him to the Areopagus, saying, "May we know what
this new teaching is that you are presenting? For you bring
some strange things to our ears. We wish to know therefore
what these things mean." Now all the Athenians and the for-
eigners who lived there would spend their time in nothing ex-
cept telling or hearing something new.

So Paul, standing in the midst of the Areopagus, said: "Men
of Athens, I perceive that in every way you are very religious. For
as I passed along and observed the objects of your worship, I
found also an altar with this inscription, 'To the unknown god.'
What therefore you worship as unknown, this I proclaim to you.
The God who made the world and everything in it, being Lord of

The glory of Athens had faded by the first century A.D. In
its prime, Athens was the cultural center of Greece. Under The-
mosticles and Pericles in the fifth century B.C., Athens became
the imperial power of its day. Its decline began in the Pelopon-
nesian War (431–404 B.C.), but much of its tradition remained
quite strong until the 6th century A.D.

heaven and earth, does not live in temples made by man, nor is he served by human hands, as though he needed anything, since he himself gives to all mankind life and breath and everything. And he made from one man every nation of mankind to live on all the face of the earth, having determined allotted periods and the boundaries of their dwelling place, that they should seek God, in the hope that they might feel their way toward him and find him. Yet he is actually not far from each one of us, for 'In him we live and move and have our being'; as even some of your own poets have said, 'For we are indeed his offspring.' Being then God's offspring, we ought not to think that the divine being is like gold or silver or stone, an image formed by the art and imagination of man. The times of ignorance God overlooked, but now he commands all people everywhere to repent, because he has fixed a day on which he will judge the world in righteousness by a man whom he has appointed; and of this he has given assurance to all by raising him from the dead."

Now when they heard of the resurrection of the dead, some mocked. But others said, "We will hear you again about this." So Paul went out from their midst. But some men joined him and believed, among them Dionysius the Areopagite and a woman named Damaris and others with them.
—Acts 17:15–34

When Paul was there, Athens was still the philosophical center of its day. Its intellectual tradition was, and arguably remains to this day, unparalleled in Western history. Socrates, who was born and raised in Athens, taught his brightest student, Plato, there. Plato later founded his Academy in Athens in 387 B.C. Plato's most famous student, Aristotle, studied there, and later founded his own school, the Lyceum, in 335 B.C. If it is true, as some have said, that the history of philosophy is just a footnote to Plato, then it is true as well that any other intellectual center in the West is a footnote to Athens. This tradition was so strong, that it was alive and well when Paul arrived there, possibly around A.D. 52.

PAUL'S PHILOSOPHICAL AUDIENCE

Two specific groups of philosophers are mentioned in our text, the Epicureans and the Stoics. There were no doubt other philosophical schools represented there that Luke does not mention, but these two were probably dominant schools of thought in Athens at this time. They were also rival schools.

The Epicureans were named after the philosopher Epicurus (341–270 B.C.). Just how much influence Epicurus actually had on the philosophy that bears his name is still debated. Their philosophy, however, was fairly straightforward. Epicureans believed that the goal (sometimes called the *telos*) of life was pleasure. This is often mistakenly thought to be a kind of crass, sensual pleasure. However, the Epicureans believed that the pleasures of the mind were always to be preferred over those of the body. They argued for the value of an intellectually detached life. According to the Epicureans, the best thing for the mind to do is to forget about this world and to think about the world above. The mind's primary focus was to be on otherworldly things.

It was wrong, therefore, to be too involved in this world, or to take matters to an extreme position, either intellectually or physically. The way to achieve maximum pleasure was to get rid of all fears, particularly fears of the gods and death. Detached from such fears, one could achieve serene pleasure in this life. One of the primary works of Epicurean philosophy was *On the Nature of Things*, by Lucretius (part of which we will look at below).

Stoicism was begun in Athens around 300 B.C. by a student of Socrates named Zeno. It took its name from the Greek word for the "porch" (*stoa*) that was originally located at the agora (marketplace). Zeno was particularly impressed by Socrates' firm resolve in the midst of difficult circumstances. This led Zeno to develop a philosophy that concentrated on one's attitude in the face of life's challenges and opportunities.

Stoics were influenced primarily by the pre-Socratic philosopher Heraclitus. Heraclitus believed that the order of the universe resulted from something he called the Logos. The Logos was thought to be a principle that provided a way for us to understand the world around us.[2] Generally speaking, Stoic philosophy taught that "God" permeated and animated all things, inexorably directing all the affairs of nature. The true Stoic learned to go along with nature and not to resist it. Once our wills are lined up with nature's path, we can become truly happy. Because of this view of nature, the Stoics have been seen as people who believe that "fate" determines the direction and details of their lives (fatalists). Since everything was predetermined, and there was nothing that they could do to change what would happen, they took a *que sera, sera* attitude—"whatever will be, will be." Life was to be tolerated, not resisted.

WHY APOLOGIZE?

We saw in chapter 1 that the Lord commands his people to do apologetics. That is our first answer to the question, Why

2. It is worth remembering that the apostle John used the idea of the Logos to describe Jesus Christ (see John 1:1, 14; 1 John 1:1–2).

apologize? In this section of Acts, though, we see another reason, one that has to do with the way we look at the world around
us. Remember that Paul was at Athens waiting for his two
friends. Since Paul had not planned to go to Athens, he could
have taken a much-needed break from his grueling schedule.
But Paul's zeal for the gospel would not let him rest. As he
walked around Athens, he became greatly distressed because
of the rampant idolatry in the city. It is likely that Paul had this
experience at Athens in mind when he later wrote to the Romans. He knew why the idols were there; he knew why the
philosophers erected and worshiped such idols—"Claiming to
be wise, they became fools, and exchanged the glory of the immortal God for images" (Romans 1:22–23). The idols were there
because the "lovers of wisdom" had foolishly suppressed the
knowledge of God. Since, as creatures made in his image, they
were not able to stop worshiping, they began to worship images
of created things.

Paul was moved by this idolatry. So, just as he had done
in other cities, he began reasoning with the Jews in the synagogue. But since he was at Athens, he also went to the agora
to reason with those who were there. There Paul met the Epicurean and Stoic philosophers, and that in turn led to his
speech at the Areopagus.

It is, in some ways, more difficult for us today to see the idols
that are worshiped in our own culture. They do not stand, as
they did at Athens, as marvelous works of art in the midst of
our cities. There are no mandates from our government to worship them. But in another way, the idols are as obvious now as
they were then for those who have eyes to see. We should not
automatically label as an idol whatever we think is unhealthy
and evil. An idol is anything that takes the place of God in some-

one's life. It is, then, something to which an unbeliever is whole-heartedly committed, not just something that is used or abused.

There are idols in every culture and in the life of every person who is rejecting the knowledge of God given in the world. Seeing those idols should motivate us to engage in apologetics. Paul was not content to hole up at the Athens Hilton until his friends arrived. He was moved to action because of what he saw in that city. It was this motivation that gave Paul an "unplanned" opportunity to defend the Christian faith.

THE PRIORITY OF PERSUASION

Before looking specifically at Paul's apology at the Areopagus, we need to understand an important element of apologetics. It is the element of persuasion. There are three basic kinds of arguments discussed in beginning logic courses. The first kind of argument is a *valid* argument. A valid argument consists of premises (initial statements) and a conclusion (a statement related to the previous ones). The validity of an argument says nothing about the truth of its premises or its conclusion. It only says that *if* the premises are true, *then* the conclusion must follow. Here is an example:

1. All horses are unicorns.
2. Black Beauty is a horse.
3. Therefore, Black Beauty is a unicorn.

This is a valid argument, even though Black Beauty is not a unicorn. As a valid argument, it simply says that *if* the first two statements are true, *then* the third one has to be true. It does not say *whether* the first two statements are true. So validity and truth are two very different things when it comes to arguments.

The next kind of argument is called a *sound* argument. In a sound argument, the premises are accepted as true. If the premises are true and the argument is valid, the conclusion must follow and be true as well. Here is an example of a sound argument:

1. All people are created in God's image.
2. Mary is a person.
3. Therefore, Mary is created in God's image.

A sound argument has one thing in common with a merely valid argument and one big difference. As in any valid argument, the conclusion in a sound argument must follow from the premises. The big difference between a sound argument and a merely valid one is that the premises are accepted as true in a sound argument.

Of course, certain premises are accepted as true by one person, but not by another. The argument above would probably not be accepted as a sound argument if we offered it to an unbeliever. He might agree to its validity, but he would not agree to its soundness, since he would reject the first premise. Since Christians would accept the two premises as true, however, the argument would be sound to them.

It is sometimes thought that what is needed in apologetics is a sound argument. If we can agree on the truth of the premises, since then the conclusion must follow, we can prove to someone that (for example) God exists. There is nothing wrong with this as it stands.

The problem, however, is that when we are discussing such vitally important matters as the existence of God or the truth of Scripture, unbelievers will rarely accept our premises. The best we can do is to present a valid argument, which says nothing about the truth of the matter.

For this reason, the next kind of argument seems to be the most critical for a biblical apologetic. This is a *persuasive* argument. We should understand that a persuasive argument does not throw out the rules of a valid or sound argument. Its design, however, is to entice the other person. It is meant to carry an appeal that neither a valid nor a sound argument is able to carry. It is meant to bring the opponent into our arena of concern.

In an apologetic context, persuasion is essential. A persuasive apologetic takes something that the non-Christian has already claimed to be true, and uses it to the advantage of the Christian defense. What separates a persuasive argument from other kinds of arguments is that, wherever possible and permissible, it incorporates the opponent's beliefs to its own advantage. This "brings the opponent in" to the discussion automatically, by affirming what he himself has said.

It also is *plausible*. This means that something is "worthy of applause." To make something plausible, then, is to present it in such a way that the other person will think it to be more likely. This is an important idea in persuasion. In attempting to make our arguments more plausible, we are being as "wise as serpents" in commending the faith.

It goes without saying that unbelievers are opposed to the gospel. For a multitude of reasons, they simply will not accept its truth. They have convinced themselves that it is something not worth believing—for them, it lacks plausibility. So, part of what we want to do in our discussion is to take what we can of what they *do* believe, and incorporate that into the truth of the gospel. In that way, we join together what they think is completely separate.

If you just present valid Christian arguments to the non-Christian, you will be met by stark disagreement. But if you adopt in your argumentation something that your opponent has agreed is true, then your other points may sound more credible.

There are two further things that should be said about persuasion as it is used in Christian apologetics. First, persuasion is an important element in Christian apologetics because of what we saw in Romans 1. People are made in God's image. We all know God. This knowledge of God is suppressed in ways that distort the truth without annihilating it. Therefore, there will be things in the life and thought of the unbeliever that will be a product of this process of suppressing the truth about God. There will be, in some ways, the truth, but it will be twisted by sin. We need to become adept at seeing those truths as twisted and then adopting them into our discussion, which will untwist them. Paul did this at Athens in various ways, as we will see below.

The second thing that we must realize is that, in the end, the Holy Spirit is the ultimate persuader. When we speak of the necessity of persuasion, we are thinking more about method than goal. Of course, it is our desire that someone actually *be* persuaded. But, in the end, we do not have the power to persuade; only God's Spirit can persuade someone of the truth of Christianity. But that should not keep us from the method itself.

This is part of the motivation of preaching. When we preach, we attempt to present the gospel in a way that will commend its truth. We could, theoretically, simply read Scripture and move on. Since God's word carries its own power and authority, we could say that our responsibility was carried out by the reading. But that would be to ignore the entire burden of Scripture's call to ministers of the gospel. It would be to ignore Christ's own method of preaching, as well as the methods of others in Scripture.

Agrippa understood well that Paul was attempting to persuade him (Acts 26:28). Paul himself tells us that part of our responsibility, as it was his, is to persuade others (2 Corinthians 5:11). We will discuss Paul's persuasive style more below. It is a central part of our apologetic. It takes thoughtful effort. It takes "premeditation" on Scripture and its truth. But it seems to be a vital approach in Scripture, so we should endeavor to make persuasion a part of our gospel communication, our preaching, and our apologetic.

PAUL'S APOLOGY

Luke tells us the actual reason why Paul was asked to address the crowd at the Areopagus. It was not that his discussions in the marketplace had been so successful; it was not that Paul was winning converts to Christ wherever he went; it was not that he was so eloquent that they wanted to hear more. Paul was invited to speak because many found him to be strange. The term that the philosophers used for Paul—"babbler" (v. 18)—was a derogatory term. The word could be more literally translated as "seed picker." In this context, it refers to someone who seems to be incoherent, grabbing intellectual "scraps" from various places and throwing them out to the public. But, as Luke tells us, the Athenians loved to spend time listening to the latest ideas, so they were intrigued by Paul's "babbling." So they brought Paul to the Areopagus—the hill of the Greek god

Ares (the Romans called him Mars)—where certain religious matters were still settled. The Areopagus was also a council of Athenians whose duties included settling certain religious and philosophical disputes.

Paul begins his apologetic by getting their attention. When he refers to them as "very religious," he purposely uses a word that is ambiguous. It is a word that could be either complimentary or critical. No doubt Paul's audience was not sure which way he meant to use the word, which is probably why he used it! There is some evidence that one was not supposed to extend compliments at the Areopagus. It was seen as a kind of bribe.

Paul uses this term, however, so that his listeners will have to listen further if they want to know what he means by it. He may be saying that they are religious people. Most who were there would have agreed with that and would have been pleased by it. Or he may be saying that they are superstitious, which they would not have wanted to hear. Paul's strategy here is to get their attention by using a term that needs clarification.

There are primarily three things that Paul accomplishes in his Areopagus apologetic. He wants his audience to know, first of all, who God is. He then wants them to understand who they are in light of this God. Finally, he wants them to understand the gospel. There can be no better summary of our own responsibility in apologetics. In defending the Christian faith, those three things should be of utmost priority in our discussions. Too often, one of them is emphasized to the neglect of the others.

Traditionally in apologetics, the discussion has focused only on the existence of God. But if that is the only topic, then the gospel is never presented as part of our defense. On the other hand, sometimes all that is discussed is the gospel itself, without attempting to wrestle with and answer the challenges that come. That too can distort the picture. And sometimes the emphasis is simply on who we are—our needs and desires. In all of these cases, there can be a distortion of our message.

We should note, however, that Paul's address is not intended to give us rigid categories. Because he discusses the existence of God, our responsibility before this God, and the gospel, we should not conclude that all of these topics should be a part of every apologetic presentation. Scripture is not giving us a mandate here. Nonetheless, in this passage we do have something of a balance of topics that should be in the forefront of our minds.

Paul begins by announcing that he will declare to them something that they have already said is unknown. That was a surprising announcement. The philosophers had intellectual abilities that were far beyond those of the general public. They used those abilities to work through the most important questions of life. We could wish that such questions were asked more often today. We could also hope that they would be asked of us.

It was the philosopher's job to answer these important questions. When answers were given, people would sit up and take notice. Few, except other philosophers, had the ability, or the luxury, to disagree with the conclusions propounded. So, philosophers would debate these important questions and then offer answers to the rest of the people.

At the Areopagus, along came Paul—not a philosopher at all, but a "seed picker"—and he boldly announced to these intellectuals that he could give them information that they had decided was unavailable. No doubt this caused the "lovers of wisdom" to take notice. No doubt some of them were agitated.

Others may have been angry. Who was this man to come and invade their turf? They had already decided that there was an unknown god; now this seed picker was claiming, not only to have knowledge of him, but to be able to declare that knowledge to them! No doubt, they were all ears by this point.

There is an apologetic lesson here that we should remember: No matter how intelligent or skilled the unbeliever is, you will always have wisdom and knowledge that he desperately needs to hear. In every case, he will need to hear the rationale for the truth of the gospel. He may be smarter. He may be the champion of the debate team. But if he is caught in unbelief, you will always know some crucial things about God, people, and the world that he could never know by his own wisdom.

Like Paul, we should not be intimidated by the abilities, impressive though they might be, of those to whom we speak. No one ever came to Christ through superior abilities. Indeed, wrote Paul to the Corinthians (just after leaving Athens):

> Where is the one who is wise? Where is the scribe? Where is the debater of this age? Has not God made foolish the wisdom of the world? For since, in the wisdom of God, the world did not know God through wisdom, it pleased God through the folly of what we preach to save those who believe. For Jews demand signs and Greeks seek wisdom, but we preach Christ crucified, a stumbling block to Jews and folly to Gentiles, but to those who are called, both Jews and Greeks, Christ the power of God and the wisdom of God. (1 Corinthians 1:20–24)

God has frustrated the wise in their wisdom. No matter how acute, that "wisdom" can never lead them to God. Only the wisdom of God in the gospel can do that. And that wisdom, received by grace through faith, belongs to all those who are in Christ.

BRASS TACKS

A couple hundred years ago, when rifles were being made in abundance, a craftsman would first determine the size and caliber of the barrel. He would then configure the stock and the lockwork. After those major elements were completed, he would consult with the buyer to see how the rifle was to be adorned or decorated. Rifles would often be embellished with brass tacks and other decorations that would make them unique. The brass tacks were the details that set each rifle apart from the others.

Now the phrase "getting down to brass tacks" has come to mean something like "getting down to the details." In Paul's Areopagus defense, Luke gives us some of the "brass tacks" of our apologetic approach. We'll mention just three, though there are others that could be noted as well.

The first "tack" to notice is Paul's understanding of God. This point cannot be overemphasized. It is most unfortunate that in our day the biblical view of God is being sacrificed for a mirage of human freedom. Many Christians are denying certain characteristics that have always been attributed to God—such as his eternity, his unchangeableness, his infinitude, and his control over all things—because these characteristics are seen as restricting human freedom or as too hard for us to understand. We should not be deceived by this trend. If we are deceived by it, we will have no defense to offer. Worse, we will in the end have no gospel to offer, either.

Paul was not afraid to begin defending his faith by mentioning God's absolute control over the universe. He knew that the Epicureans and the Stoics had their own theories about the universe. But he also knew that they used those theories to suppress what they actually knew (but would not acknowledge). So, Paul begins his defense by telling his listeners what they already know. As we saw in the last two chapters, they already knew God. They knew *the* God. And their altar dedicated to an unknown God was not an attempt to find God, but to hide from the one they knew.

So Paul began by reminding them of what God had been telling them all along through the created world:

> The God who made the world and everything in it, being Lord of heaven and earth, does not live in temples made by man, nor is he served by human hands, as though he needed anything. (Acts 17:24–25)

God is the Creator. As Creator, he is Lord. The two go hand in hand. Since he created all things, he rules all things. And, says Paul, since he created all things, he needs nothing.

Paul goes on to tell them that God "made from one man every nation of mankind to live on all the face of the earth, having determined allotted periods and the boundaries of their dwelling place" (v. 26). In a word, Paul begins by emphasizing the sovereignty of God. We may not need to stress this point in every apologetic discussion, but we should always remember its central truth. The sovereignty of God must not be compromised or watered down for the sake of convenience or to avoid offense. It is the one truth that challenges sinners—sinners who themselves want to be little sovereigns.

Since God rules over what he has made, he is not in need of anything. I well remember a gospel presentation I heard years ago. At the conclusion of the message, the man said to his audience, "I want to play a song for you. I want you to think of this song as your song to God." He then played a song entitled "You Needed Me." It is hard to imagine a presentation more opposed to gospel truth.

This is not a new problem. Even ancient Israel became convinced at one point that God was in need of them and their sacrifices. So the Lord came and rebuked Israel for her disobedience:

> I will not accept a bull from your house or goats from your folds. For every beast of the forest is mine, the cattle on a thousand hills. . . . If I were hungry, I would not tell you, for the world and its fullness are mine. Do I eat the flesh of bulls or drink the blood of goats? (Psalm 50:9–13)

Israel, in her rebellion and wickedness, had convinced herself that God was actually in need of her sacrifices. They had envisioned a god who got hungry. That God, like the "unknown god" of the philosophers, was an idol.

Any god who is not sovereign is an idol. Paul knows that, so he attacks the idolatry at its root. He declares God to be sovereign. With that declaration, there is no room for idols.

Paul's second "tack" is to remind his listeners who they are before this sovereign God. They are the ones who came from "one man" (v. 26). They live in the presence of God (v. 27). As a matter of fact, they "live and move and have [their] being" *in* this God (v. 28). This is Paul's application of the sovereignty of God to their lives. It is not just that God rules from on high (since he cannot live in temples made by man—v. 24), but that his rule as Lord is ever before his creation. It is ever before us, his creatures.

This is just another way of saying what Paul says in Romans. Since God is actively revealing himself in all of creation, he is present in and with that creation. This means that all people live their lives before the face of God. It also means that, for people to be people at all, they must live, move, and exist *in God*. In other words, their lives and very existence depend on God. The hymn writer put it this way:

> There's not a plant or flow'r below
> But makes your glories known
> And clouds arise and tempests blow
> By order from your throne;
> While all that borrows life from you
> Is ever in your care,
> And everywhere that man can be,
> You, God, are present there.
>
>   (William Cowper)

It will help us greatly to remember our dependence on God in our apologetic discussions. While the people in Paul's audience did not acknowledge it, that did not keep Paul from reminding them of it. Paul was appealing to what he knew to be true in their lives and hearts. They lived, as God's creatures, before his face.

The eighteenth-century American theologian Jonathan Edwards had trouble with the notion of hell as "the absence of God." He had trouble with that notion because he knew that God is not really absent from any part of his creation (see Psalm

139). Instead, said Edwards, we ought to think of hell as the very presence of God.

But what would make the presence of God hell? We could think of it like this. Given what Paul says in Romans and in this section of Acts, every person knows God, but spends a lot of effort denying that knowledge. Every person lives, moves, and exists in God, but will not acknowledge that fact. So for a person who had suppressed his knowledge in God, to spend eternity face-to-face with God would be utter torment. To face the one who gave you all good things, but for which you would not give thanks (Romans 1:19), and against whom you constantly rebelled, would be torment.

This is one of the reasons why Paul makes the point that he does here. He wants his audience to know that the sovereign God is not someone who is beyond reach or beyond knowing. The philosophers did not claim that this god was unknowable because he was so far off. They said he was unknowable because they would not see the obvious.

The third "tack" for Paul is the truth of the gospel. There is little question that what Luke records for us here is an edited speech. We do not have all that Paul said on Mars Hill. But we do have a summary of his gospel presentation. He does not stop with the character of God or with our response to God. He concludes his address by calling his listeners to repentance:

> The times of ignorance God overlooked, but now he commands all people everywhere to repent, because he has fixed a day on which he will judge the world in righteousness by a man whom he has appointed; and of this he has given assurance to all by raising him from the dead. (Acts 17:30–31)

Judgment will come, Paul reminds the Athenians. It will come through Jesus Christ. The only escape from that judgment is to repent.

No doubt many in the audience believed that history was like a circle. Round and round it goes, and where it stops, nobody knows. We die, and then we come back again as something or someone else. But Paul tells them that history will end. It does not go around and around, but is moving toward a specific end. That end is the return of Jesus Christ. The Christ who was crucified is now raised, and he will come again. He will come again, not as Savior, but as Lord and Judge of the world.

This was now the opportunity for Paul's listeners to respond in repentance. But did they?

THE SECRET OF SUCCESS

There has been much discussion of Paul's address at the Areopagus. Some have said that Paul was so discouraged after this that, when he went to Corinth, he decided to stop reasoning and to do nothing more than preach "Jesus Christ and him crucified" (1 Corinthians 2:2). This, however, seems to miss Paul's own emphasis in ministry.

But how should we measure Paul's success on Mars Hill? How do you know if you have been successful in giving your defense of Christianity? Notice the reaction to Paul's address:

> Now when they heard of the resurrection of the dead, some mocked. But others said, "We will hear you again about this." So Paul went out from their midst. But some men joined him and believed, among them

Dionysius the Areopagite and a woman named Damaris and others with them. (Acts 17:32–34)

Was that response indicative of success?

By some standards, no. But we must remember what our goal is in apologetics. Although we should desire and pray for conversions, it is not our goal in apologetics to convert others; nor is it to win the argument. Only God can produce conversions. Our goal in apologetics is simply to tell the truth in a biblical way. If we do that, we have been successful in the eyes of God.

We should not be intent on "winning" the argument. That seems to be foreign to biblical thinking. We could be so consumed with winning the argument, that we either communicate the gospel in an offensive way or neglect to communicate it at all. The gospel carries its own offense (2 Corinthians 2:15–16). It is not our job to add offense to it.

THE ATHENIAN "CONNECTION" — MORE ON PERSUASION

There is one more important element in this passage that deserves special attention because of its importance in apologetics. As we noted above, it is especially important because it is undervalued in apologetics today. We are referring to Paul's masterful means of persuasion.

We have already seen Paul's emphasis on the sovereignty of God. Given that emphasis, Paul would never have thought that someone could be argued or persuaded into the truth of the gospel. Having said that, however, we should not conclude that argument and persuasion are not important in our defense and communication of the faith. While those elements may not have the power to convert someone to Christ, God can use them for his own wise purposes, and he often does use them in conversion (see Isaiah 55:10–11; Romans 10:12–15).

The word *persuade* means something like "to urge thoroughly." It involves much more than just telling the truth, although it includes that. Typically, when we talk about persuading someone, we are talking about a way of telling the truth.

For example, suppose I would like for you to visit my favorite restaurant. I would like for you to eat there because I am convinced that you would enjoy the meals there as much as I do. I could tell you the truth about the restaurant if I said to you, "You should visit this restaurant. They have good food there." That would be true enough, but there isn't much of persuasive value in that description.

But suppose I said, "I am convinced that you would love this restaurant. I know that you love filet mignon with béarnaise sauce. This restaurant uses only black angus beef, and each of their filets is a minimum of two inches thick, cooked to perfection. Their béarnaise is the lightest, richest sauce I have ever tasted. They seat you in a private room overlooking the water. . . ." You get the idea?

In both cases, I am telling the truth. In the latter case, however, there is a strong persuasive element. That element can be summed up in one word—*connection*. The key component in my pitch for the restaurant was in the statement, "I know that you love filet mignon with béarnaise sauce." Had I known nothing of the tastes of the person to whom I was speaking, persuasion would have been nearly impossible.

But we do know something, in fact many things, about our unbelieving friends. The last two chapters were meant to spell out some of the things we know. Whenever we are attempting to defend and commend the Christian faith, we are trying to convince them of the truth of what we believe. The best way to do that is to use what we know of their own beliefs as tools for persuasion.

This was Paul's approach at the Areopagus. It should not surprise us that the apostle Paul was a master at persuasion. How did Paul go about "urging thoroughly" on Mars Hill? As a master intellect himself, Paul had the advantage of knowing his audience rather thoroughly. While this is not absolutely necessary in order to make a persuasive argument, it does seem to be true that the better we know our audience, the better our persuasion can be.

We have an excellent example of the kind of persuasion that we should try to imitate in verses 24–27. In those verses, Paul is telling his hearers what kind of God this is that they have mistakenly labeled as unknown. One of the reasons that Paul describes God as he does is that the true God shares many of the characteristics that the philosophers themselves attributed to other gods. So Paul is using their own words, their own ideas, as a kind of hook, both to pull them in and to show them their error.

For example, as Paul begins to argue with the philosophers about the nature of God, he uses terminology with which most of them would be familiar. Both Zeno and Euripides had argued that the divine was not able to be contained by human temples: "What house fashioned by builders can contain the divine form within enclosing walls?"[3] Paul likely knew this, so

---

3. Joseph A. Fitzmyer, S. J., "The Acts of the Apostles: A New Translation with Introduction and Commentary," in *The Anchor Bible,* vol. 31 (New York: Doubleday, 1997), 608.

in his description of the true God, he reminded them, "The God who made the world and everything in it, being Lord of heaven and earth, does not live in temples made by man" (v. 24). They agreed that some of their gods did not dwell here; Paul is telling them that in fact the true God does not dwell here.

Now Paul could easily have come to these philosophers and said, "Euripides is a pagan. He is in gross error in his understanding and description of God." That would have been true. Since Euripides' god was an idol, any description of him (it?) would have been wrong. But Paul was as wise as a serpent and as innocent as a dove (Matthew 10:16). He knew that it would be more effective to use ideas that the philosophers already agreed to. So, he took those ideas and brought them back into their proper context. He redefined them as Christian ideas.

It is important to notice that Paul was not saying that his audience was right in their understanding of God. Although Paul was yet to write the epistle to the Romans, he no doubt knew its principles well! He knew that the understanding that his audience had of God was always "truth with a twist."

Instead of just telling the truth, therefore, Paul takes their twisted (suppressed) notions of an unknown God and begins to unravel them. Like a master puzzler, Paul takes the scattered, confused, and chaotic bits and pieces of his audience's knowledge and places them in the proper order and in the proper frame.

But in using and redefining their ideas, Paul is also telling them much more than what they had thought. He uses their own concepts as elements of persuasion, but he also says, from the very start, that this God, who does not dwell in human temples, is the Lord and Creator of all things. Paul uses some of their own ideas, but he places them into the Christian context of the Creator God who rules over all.

This notion of God's lordship would have been foreign to the Stoics in particular. The supreme principle in Stoic philosophy was impersonal. As Paul presents God as Creator and Lord, he is affirming that God is personal, not impersonal, and that he is in fact the supreme person.

More persuasion is used in verse 25. Paul reminds his hearers that this personal God is not dependent on anything at all. God needs nothing. Again, this was not a new idea for these philosophers. Lucretius had said, "The very nature of divinity must necessarily enjoy immortal life in the deepest peace, far removed and separated from our troubles; for without any pain, without danger, itself mighty by its own resources, needing us not at all. . . ."[4]

The philosophers had their own idea of an independent god (or gods). Paul includes that idea, again, as a point of persuasion. He does not simply say to them that Lucretius's idea of independence was a pagan notion. That would have been true. But it would have lacked any persuasive value. Instead, he affirms that God is not in need of anything, even as Lucretius had said.

But he also tells them that this independent God is not as detached as they thought he was. He gives to all creatures life and breath and everything else. That is, this God is no abstract deity. He is not "withdrawn from our affairs . . . , detached, afar"; rather, he acts in history to sustain our lives at each moment. He is as close to us as our very lives.

4. Lucretius, "De Rerum Natura," trans. W. H. D. Rouse, in The Loeb Classical Library, ed. T. E. Page (Cambridge, Mass.: Harvard University Press, 1959), 131.

So, in using elements of persuasion, Paul is not afraid to disagree with them as well. He implements elements of persuasion when he can, and without compromising the truth of the
faith, but he also disagrees with them when he must.

Note another example. The Stoics, some of whom were
there on Mars Hill, had a notion that the world was predetermined. The best life, they taught, is the one that accepts that
predetermination and does not resist it. Acceptance should then
bring about a detached peace in us.

Paul agrees that God, this God whom the philosophers had
declared to be unknown, determines our lives (v. 26). But the
philosophers could not reconcile the fact of this abstract, determining, independent God with a notion of involvement with
the world. If God were independent, then he could not be involved with the world, because then he would be in some sense
dependent on it. Paul, again, as a master apologist, argues that
both things are true. And, as a master apologist, he uses words
from other philosophers to prove his point.

Two Greek poets are quoted by Paul in this Areopagus address (v. 28). The first quote is from Epimenides of Crete, whom
Paul quotes again in Titus 1:12. Epimenides notes of Zeus that
it is "in him that we live, and move and exist." The other poet
quoted is Aratus, who notes that we are all "his offspring."[5]

Again, there are at least two ways to deal with this. One
way, the way that Paul does not choose, is simply to tell the Athenians that they have it all wrong. Paul could have stood up and,
rightly and truthfully, denounced their loyalty to Zeus and
called them all idolaters. Given that it was idolatry that moved
him to speak on this occasion, that is what we might have
expected.

5. See, for example, Fitzmyer, "Acts of the Apostles," 610f.

But Paul doesn't do that, and here again we see the wisdom of his apologetic. Instead, he quotes those poets, using statements that would have been familiar to his entire audience. But notice how he quotes them. It is sometimes thought that Paul is agreeing that these Greek poets are at least partly right. All that Paul is doing, it is often thought, is adding the gospel to the Greek's proper notion of God. But that is not what Paul is doing at all. Remember that he knows the source of his audience's beliefs. He knows that these beliefs are "twisted truths" that come from sinful reactions to God's natural revelation. As such, they are, in the hands of the Greeks, condemnable. They are in error. The Greeks would be without excuse if they stood before God with these notions. When they died, they would not be able to say to God, "See, we got it half right!" In that sense, the things that they believed were simply not true at all.

When Epimenides says that "in him" we live and move and exist, he does not have the true God in mind at all. He is writing about a god of his own creation, a false god. When Aratus says that we are "his" offspring, he is not referring to the true God, but to Zeus. And it simply is not true that we are the offspring of Zeus. These twisted truths have become foolish exchanges of the truth of God for a lie.

But, when taken back to their rightful place, to the context of Christianity, these are glorious truths. So Paul takes them back. The Greeks had used these ideas to suppress the true knowledge of God. Paul takes them back to communicate the truth about the true Creator and Lord. In that sense Paul is saying, "Your ideas and concepts can only be true if they refer to the true God."

Once placed in their proper context, these ideas of the Greek philosophers come back to their rightful place as absolute truths about the Christian God. That is Paul's point, which he offers as a point of persuasion in his defense of Christianity.

A powerful statement made in verse 29 can be seen as, in some ways, the climax of Paul's argument. It is theologically packed and apologetically persuasive. Notice Paul's reasoning.

He has just used the Athenians' own words to describe to them this "unknown" deity, the God of Christianity. Now he uses those same words, again brought back into their proper context, to counter their idolatry. Since it is the case, he says, that we are God's offspring, how can we think that God is like inanimate things made by us? This is really Paul's persuasive masterstroke. In this one statement, he shows the wisdom of the world to be, in fact, foolishness.

Remember that the philosophers prided themselves on their wisdom. Their intellects were thought to be beyond compare. That was true *especially* at Athens. So Paul's rebuke here was all the more embarrassing. He told them something that would be obvious to even the most uneducated.

For those familiar with Detective Columbo, Paul's statement here is similar to Columbo's "one more question" just before he traps the killer. To put it in the form of a question, Paul is saying, "Could I ask just one more question of you philosophers? Given that you say that we are God's offspring, how can you also believe that God is something you yourselves have made? Wouldn't that mean that God is your offspring?" To think that God is like things that we make, while believing that we are something that he has made, seems to be an obvious intellectual blunder. Has not God made foolish the wisdom of the world?

Paul is appealing here to creatures made in the image of God. He is doing so in at least two ways. First, he is appealing to the image of God in arguing that we human beings are God's offspring. In that way, we bear some kind of resemblance to him. But he is also appealing to the image of God in the sense that we saw in Romans 1. He is telling the Athenians that their idol making goes against what they know to be the case. It goes against what they know about God; it goes against their own reasoning about God. If we are his offspring, then we are more like him than any gold or silver thing that we could make.

Here again Paul is appealing to the fact that God is personal. He is not something that animates all things and creates motion in them, as some of his audience believed. Rather, he is the sovereign, independent Creator and Lord, who sustains all things in this world *and whose offspring we are!* This moves Paul's audience from a consideration of God to a consideration of who we are in relation to God, and it does so by using the very things that the Greeks themselves had said!

From this point, Paul moves to a presentation of the gospel. In this presentation, he refutes both the Epicureans' and the Stoics' beliefs about fear and judgment and the afterlife. While they disagreed with each other on many points, they both agreed that the best attitude toward life was one of detachment from it. The Epicureans, specifically, saw the fear of the afterlife as one of the main obstacles to that detachment, so they attempted to deny it altogether. In his defense of Christ's resurrection, Paul is now moving to more of a head-on confrontation. He is telling them that they must repent, because this God will come to judge the world. His judgment will be through Jesus Christ, who was raised from the dead. Since he was raised, he is alive, and he will come back.

This likely threw the audience into disarray. There must have been a good bit of conversation going on as Paul uttered these words. He was telling them that they were to turn around and trust Christ. But notice again that Paul was not simply saying that. He had already laid the groundwork to say such a radical thing. He was saying that this God, whose offspring we are, will come back in his Son. His Son was raised from the dead and has been appointed to judge the world in righteousness. The proof that he will do so lies in his resurrection.

Remember, the goal of apologetics, just like the goal of evangelism and preaching, is to tell the truth. This is a goal that we can, by God's grace, accomplish. We must be truthful in our apologetic because we are appealing to the truth that the unbeliever already knows. Our "point of connection," or of persuasion, with the unbeliever is the truth that God has given to him. Like Paul, we might see how the unbeliever has perverted that truth. Given what Paul says in Romans 1, we should expect to see ideas and actions that are a twisting of the truth that God has provided to them. In appealing to that, we make our apologetic hit home. As truth, it comes immediately into contact with the truth that God has given to them in nature. It speaks, therefore, to their very hearts. It screams its truth in their inner souls.

This is our goal. This goal should be pursued as we speak to unbelievers about God, about who they are, and about what Christ has done. Paul was not discouraged at Athens. How could he be discouraged when, despite the sneers and jeers, "some men joined him and believed, among them Dionysius the Areopagite and a woman named Damaris and others with them" (v. 34)?

Paul saw the conversion of a few there that day—even one man on the council was converted. But even if he had seen no conversions, Paul knew well that his ministry was a service, a service to Jesus Christ. Christ would bring in his own as Paul

went from place to place, reasoning in the synagogues and in
the marketplace, telling his audiences the truth—the truth that
is in Jesus Christ alone. Paul's defense of the faith was a commending of Christ. And his commending of Christ was itself a
defense. Any defense of the Christian faith is meant to be a defense of the faith that is in Christ Jesus our Lord.

Set him apart as Lord—and be ready. The battle is the
Lord's!

DIGGING DEEPER

1. What can we learn from Paul's motivation to defend the
   faith in Acts 17:16?
2. What are some differences between proof and persuasion?
3. What are some of the most crucial things that we should
   know about God as we defend Christianity?
4. How do you know if your defense of the gospel is
   successful?
5. What elements of society, culture, or unbelief generally
   could you use as elements of persuasion in an apologetic
   conversation?

CONCLUSION

WE SHOULD NOW be better acquainted with the ideas in the summary paragraph that we read in the introduction:

> Since Christ is Lord, and the battle is his, we must always be ready to contend for the faith once for all delivered to the saints. We must use the weapons, not of this world, but of the Lord. We must take every thought captive to the obedience of Christ as we demolish the arguments, with gentleness and reverence, of those who suppress the truth in unrighteousness, exchanging the truth of God for a lie, worshiping created things, rather than the Creator, who is blessed forever. Amen.

Jesus Christ is the Lord. That truth should guide the entirety of our Christian thinking and living. It should guide our apologetic endeavors as well. Since he is Lord, the battle is his. Everything is his; he owns the cattle on a thousand hills. But because the battle is his, it is to be fought with him as the commander. It is to be fought his way, using his weapons, that he might be glorified in the midst of the battle. If it is fought with those things in mind, success is inevitable, even if we cannot see it.

We prepare ourselves for Christ's battle by becoming familiar with his Word. As we have seen, this means that we should know his Word, but it also means that we should think of its truth in the context of the culture around us, and of challenges that come our way. The Word of God is meant to be an encouragement to us.

But it is also meant to provide answers to and for those who would try to deny its power. Like Goliath, there are many who would taunt the Lord and pretend that his power is a fiction. We must respond in faith, like David, and seek to apply the sword of the Spirit in order to penetrate to the deep recesses of unbelieving hearts.

To know God's Word in this way is to begin to take every thought captive to the obedience of Christ. It is to begin to develop a way of seeing the world, to incorporate all that we know of the invisible world into our interpretation and understanding of the visible world. In that way, like the saints of old, we begin to see the unseen (see Hebrews 11). We are then being transformed by the renewing of our minds (Romans 12:2).

All of this is accomplished, if done in faith, with gentleness and reverence. A significant part of thinking through the Word of God, answering challenges to our faith, is that we take on the attitude of Christ himself (Philippians 2:1–2). We speak in humility, with reverence, knowing that we too would be caught in unbelief if it were not for the gracious work of the triune God, who changed us and made us his own.

God has ensured that all of his creatures would know him. Although that knowledge is suppressed, it cannot be erased completely. Much that the unbeliever does and thinks has the knowledge of God at its root. Much of the sin that enslaves the unbeliever is evidence of God's wrath, which is poured out just because of the refusal to acknowledge God. The universe that God has made—everything it contains—is abundant evidence of who God is and what he requires of all who are made in his image.

So, we are to take advantage of the marvelous privilege of fighting the Lord's battles, with his weapons, in his way. In fighting those battles, we must never lose sight of whose battle it is. We fight the Lord's battles, in the words of David, "that all this assembly may know that the LORD saves not with sword and spear. For the battle is the LORD's, and he will give you into our hand" (1 Samuel 17:47).

APOLOGETICS
AND THE HOLY SPIRIT

"NO ONE CAN BE argued into the kingdom." Have you ever heard that? Maybe you have, or maybe you have made such a statement yourself. That statement, perhaps more than any other, is one reason given for the uselessness of the apologetic task.

Since no one can be argued into heaven, we're sometimes told, to spend our time thinking through or working on arguments or answers is a fruitless endeavor. Not only can no one be argued into the kingdom, but Jesus himself encouraged us not to spend time on what we should say in the face of challenges to our faith:

> But before all this they will lay their hands on you and persecute you, delivering you up to the synagogues and prisons, and you will be brought before kings and governors for my name's sake. This will be your opportu-

nity to bear witness. Settle it therefore in your minds
not to meditate beforehand how to answer, for I will
give you a mouth and wisdom, which none of your adversaries will be able to withstand or contradict. (Luke
21:12–15)

This passage, like related passages in Matthew and Mark,
seems to discourage any preparation for, or concern about,
apologetics. The Greek word that Luke uses for the phrase
"how to answer" comes from the verb *apologeomai,* from which
we get our word *apologetics.* It looks as though Christ is telling
us not to prepare for the apologetic task.

Is Jesus commanding his disciples not to be ready to defend
their faith? Is he telling them that they need not prepare for
challenges to the faith that will come their way? Because this
passage can be easily misunderstood, we should look at it carefully as we think about the apologetic task.

It will be helpful, first of all, to look at the role of the Holy
Spirit in the world generally, and then to see how crucial his
work is when we are called on to defend our faith.

We should first remember just what it is that the Holy Spirit
came to do after Christ's ascension. Jesus was very specific about
this in his Upper Room discourse as recorded for us in the gospel
of John. We understand, first of all in this discourse, that the
Holy Spirit could not come unless Jesus himself went away.
This is crucial to understand and is sometimes overlooked. Jesus
is making a new covenant point.

In the old covenant, the people of God were confined,
roughly, to the nation of Israel. God's redemptive work had its
focus among them. The work of God was confined in the old
covenant in a way that it is not in the new. But the old covenant
was always pointing to the new covenant. It did not come as a

surprise or an afterthought in the plan of God. Even as far back as Genesis, when the Lord announced his covenant plan to Abram, God's intent was clearly to move beyond the nation of Israel:

> When Abram was ninety-nine years old the LORD appeared to Abram and said to him, "I am God Almighty; walk before me, and be blameless, that I may make my covenant between me and you, and may multiply you greatly." Then Abram fell on his face. And God said to him, "Behold, my covenant is with you, *and you shall be the father of a multitude of nations."* (Genesis 17:1–4)

The Lord's intent for the salvation of his people, even from the beginning, included many nations, not just the nation of Israel. Later on in Israel's history, the Lord made the nature of his new covenant even clearer:

> I will give you a new heart, and a new spirit I will put within you. And I will remove the heart of stone from your flesh and give you a heart of flesh. And I will put my Spirit within you, and cause you to walk in my statutes and be careful to obey my rules. (Ezekiel 36:26–27)

The new covenant would include more than Israel:

> Worthy are you to take the scroll and to open its seals, for you were slain, and by your blood *you ransomed people for God from every tribe and language and people and nation,* and you have made them a kingdom and

priests to our God, and they shall reign on the earth.
(Revelation 5:9–10)

The fulfillment of the history of redemption came in Jesus
Christ. Jesus came, not to be served, but to serve and to give his
life as a ransom for many (Mark 10:45). He came to die. That
was his mission. He came to die so that he might be raised from
the dead (Romans 1:4) and exalted to the right hand of the Father (Hebrews 1:2).

We often miss, however, the point of Jesus' words to his disciples in the Upper Room. He told them that it was necessary
for him to go away. It was necessary because the Holy Spirit
would not come until Christ went away.

It was on the Day of Pentecost that the redemptive, once-
for-all work of Jesus concluded. On that day, *it was Jesus who
baptized with the Holy Spirit.* This was the message of John the
Baptist: *"He* will baptize you with the Holy Spirit and with fire"
(Matthew 3:11). The point that John is making here is not to
tell us what the Holy Spirit would do at Pentecost. Rather, it is
to tell us what Christ would do on that day. When Christ tells
his disciples that he must go away so that the Holy Spirit will
come, he is telling them that he must go away to complete his
once-for-all work for his people. He must go away in order to
fulfill the Scriptures—the *old covenant* Scriptures—which speak
of the coming of the Spirit.

Christ promised to send the Spirit (John 16:7). He also told
the disciples what the Spirit would do. He would convict the
world concerning sin, righteousness, and judgment. These three
things are essential elements of the gospel. The Holy Spirit
comes to work in and through the proclamation of the gospel
to convict the world. This is a part of his ministry from the Day

of Pentecost to the end of the age. He is sent by Christ on Pentecost for that purpose.

There is much more that Christ wants to tell his disciples in that Upper Room, but he spares them the painful details. Those details, he says, will be left to the Spirit when he comes.

Notice what Jesus says next. In one sense, he gives us a summary of the Spirit's entire ministry. He says to his disciples, "He will glorify me" (John 16:14). The Spirit was not sent here to create or establish a ministry that was in some way more than or different from the ministry of Christ. The Spirit's ministry is to glorify Christ. That means that the Spirit was sent to point to, to call attention to, to declare the ministry of, Jesus Christ. That means, among other things, that any ministry focused on the Holy Spirit himself is not a part of the ministry of the Spirit. It is the ministry of Christ that the Spirit highlights. He was sent for that reason.

This ministry of glorifying Christ takes on a specifically apostolic character. Jesus says not only that the Spirit "will glorify me," but also, more specifically: "He will glorify me, for he will take what is mine and declare it to you" (v. 14). This refers specifically to the work of the Spirit in revealing the word of Christ to the disciples. One of the primary activities of the Spirit's ministry after Christ's ascension was his focus on bringing to completion the word of Christ.

There are three different aspects to the Spirit's ministry with and through Christ's word that we should highlight here. The first work of the Spirit with the Word is what we might call his work of inspiration. Here we understand that it was the Spirit of God who moved men to write the very words of God in Scripture. "All Scripture is breathed out by God," Paul told Timothy (2 Timothy 3:16).

The Greek word that Paul uses for "breathed out by God" means that all Scripture came to us as a product of the Spirit's work through the Lord's prophets and apostles. It came over time, in history, and it came to completion. So this was a "seasonal" work of the Spirit, in that it was necessary for a time, but was not a work that the Spirit continues today. It was necessary so that the Bible as we have it would be a closed book. There is no revelation to be added to it. There is none to be taken away.

The Spirit's work was to glorify Christ by giving his disciples the words to write for the church through the ages. This is what Christ meant when he said to the disciples, "He [the Holy Spirit] will guide you into all the truth" (John 16:13).

Is this what Christ means in the passage above in Luke 21, where he cautions his disciples about how they should act when brought before the authorities? It may very well be. It may be that Christ is giving special instructions to his disciples, *as his disciples,* that would not apply to us in the same way. This would not be a new idea in Scripture at all. It fits very well with the way in which the Spirit worked in the old covenant (Old Testament).

Just after the Lord called Moses to free his people from Egypt, he promised Moses, "I will . . . teach you what you shall speak" (Exodus 4:12). The Lord's call to Jeremiah included the encouragement, "I have put my words in your mouth" (Jeremiah 1:9). It is in keeping with the Lord's call of men to special, prophetic ministries that he promises the disciples that he will give them words to say.

It may be, however, that Christ's instruction was meant first for his disciples, but after that for the church as well. If it was meant for the church as well, the Lord is telling us that it is *his* word that should be our focus when we are challenged. More on that below.

In any case, it is important to see what Christ is not saying. He is not saying that the disciples, or we, should not prepare ourselves at all for a confrontation with those who oppose him. The integrity of Scripture will not allow for such an interpretation. If that is what Christ is saying, then Peter and others explicitly contradict him when they command us to prepare ourselves to give an answer. Since it is the same Spirit who inspired these and all other texts of Scripture, that option is not open to the Christian.

It seems likely that Christ is saying something similar to what we saw in chapter 1. There we remember that Peter was saying to those scattered Christians that they should not "fear what they fear" and should not be frightened. This is the burden of Christ's charge to his followers. We are not to be anxious, nor to fear in the way that the world fears. Instead, continues Peter, we are to set Christ apart as Lord. Just as Christ commands his disciples not to worry, but to trust, so Peter commands us not to fear, but to sanctify the lordship of Christ in our hearts.

The second aspect of the Spirit's ministry is what we might call his work of synergy ("working with"). The Spirit works with Christ's word, which we find in the Bible. This is the work that the Spirit does as he speaks in and through the Word itself. This is one of those truths that could easily revolutionize our practice of apologetics, of preaching, and of evangelism. This work of the Spirit is well expressed in the Westminster Confession of Faith:

> The supreme judge by which all controversies of religion are to be determined, and all decrees of councils,

> opinions of ancient writers, doctrines of men, and private spirits, are to be examined, and in whose sentence we are to rest, can be no other but *the Holy Spirit speaking in the Scripture*. (1.10 [emphasis added])

This last phrase, "the Holy Spirit speaking in Scripture," emphasizes that we should never think that God the Holy Spirit works independently of the truth of God's Word, or that the Word goes out without the Spirit.

For example, it is often said among well-meaning Christians that "the Lord told them" what they must do, or say, or how they must act. We need to understand that with the finished work of Christ came the finished work of Christ's word (see Hebrews 1:1–4). Thus, the Holy Spirit does not speak to people, even to his people, apart from the word of Christ in the Bible. Hebrews does remind us that, in days gone by, God did speak through his appointed representatives—"by the prophets." But he has ceased speaking in that way.

In these last days, he has spoken to us through his Son. The completion of the Son's work marks the completion of his word as well. But that does not mean that his word is dead. Part of the Spirit's ministry in glorifying Christ is to speak through his word in the Bible.

On the other hand, we should avoid thinking of God's Word simply as a text without a living testimony. We should see the words of Scripture as alive; they are the words of a living God, who is speaking to us through them. Viewed in that way, our study of Scripture could never be a simple matter of gathering facts.

Scripture is God's completed "conversation" with us about who he is and what he has done in and through his Son. As the hymn writer put it, "What more can he say than to you he has said?" He has said all he needs to say in his Word. With the Spirit speaking in that Word, it is never a dead letter, but is life itself to us. "The highest proof of Scripture," according to John Calvin, "derives in general from the fact that God in person speaks in it."[1]

The third aspect of the Spirit's ministry is his work of testimony. I remember talking to a young man about the gospel one day. As I talked, he affirmed all that I said. He believed that Christ had come, had died on the cross for sins, and had risen again. He believed that he had sinned and could not get to heaven on his own. Toward the end of this discussion, he turned to me and said, "Yes, I believe all this, but so what?"

It is not enough simply to believe *that* Christ came, died on the cross for sins, etc. We must believe *in* Christ. To believe *that* Christ came, etc., is to believe that certain statements are true. It's like believing *that* my father could catch me if I jumped down from a cliff, or believing *that* my mother will not poison me at supper tonight.

But to believe *in* my father or *in* my mother would mean to jump so my father could catch me, or to eat the dinner that my mother fixed. To believe *in* someone means to put our very lives into their hands. It means to follow their instructions, to trust that what they are doing is needful and not harmful to us.

The only way to move from "believing that" to "believing in" is by the testimony of the Holy Spirit. The Spirit speaking in Scripture is crucial. It is a necessary element of Scripture as it brings together the authority of God's word with his activity in the world. But it will not change a sinful heart. Sinful hearts

---

1. John Calvin, *Institutes of the Christian Religion,* ed. John T. McNeill, trans. Ford Lewis Battles (Philadelphia: Westminster Press, 1960), 1.7.4.

need supernatural work. That work is the testimony of the Holy Spirit.

The testimony of the Holy Spirit provides an answer to "So what?" It assures me that I am in desperate need of a Savior, that the death of Christ on the cross was for *my* sins, that the most important thing in my life is to glorify and please God, that I am his child and he will never leave me or forsake me, etc.

Without the testimony of the Spirit, I may agree to these things; I may believe *that* they are true, but I will not, I cannot, believe *in* them. I will not put my life into the everlasting arms of Christ unless his Spirit testifies to me, changing my heart, so that my love for him overshadows everything else. "So what?" will be answered only if and when the Spirit testifies to the truth of the gospel.

The testimony of the Spirit gives us an assurance that can only come from above—the assurance that God is for us and that, therefore, no one can ultimately stand against us (Romans 8:31). It tells us that we are children of God (see Romans 8:15–16). Again, according to John Calvin:

> If we desire to provide in the best way for our consciences—that they may not be perpetually beset by the instability of doubt or vacillation, and that they may not also boggle at the smallest quibbles—we ought to seek our conviction in a higher place than human reasons, judgments, or conjectures, that is, in the secret testimony of the Spirit.[2]

2. Ibid.

So how should we understand Jesus' words in Luke 21? We should notice three things about this passage.

First, the kind of situation that Jesus describes is apologetic in nature. "There will come a time," Jesus is telling his disciples, "when you will have an opportunity to bear witness of me. You will be brought before the authorities because of your Christian faith."

This is a situation that is foreign to most of us. The ruling authorities, at least in most of the West, have not made Christianity illegal (yet). But it was not foreign to first- and second-century Christians. One of the first apologists of the second century, Justin Martyr, was called on to defend his faith, and the faith of his brothers and sisters in Christ, in the presence of the emperor. He knew what it meant to be brought before the governing authorities because of his faith in Christ. And he knew that he might lose his life as he sought to commend the faith to the emperor.

While we may not, in our lifetime, be called before the rulers, the same principles hold. Whenever we are challenged, or our faith is questioned, we are in an apologetic situation. It is time, at that point, to defend and commend the faith.

Second, Jesus' command in Luke 21:14 "not to meditate beforehand" may seem at first to run counter to other passages we have seen. Why would Peter ask us always to be "prepared," but Jesus tell his disciples "not to meditate beforehand" about the coming challenges?

We should notice, first of all, that the parallel passages in both Matthew and Mark use a different verb. In both cases, they use the verb "to be anxious" (Matthew 10:19) or "to be anxious beforehand" (Mark 13:11). Because these three gospels were written, in part, to give us different perspectives on the same event, Matthew and Mark can help us understand Jesus' concern for his disciples.

Jesus was telling his disciples that they were not to be anxious, or to worry, about the various rules, laws, and customs that might cause a conflict with their testimonies. He was telling them that they wouldn't need to be legal experts or familiar with every jot and tittle of Roman customs. They were not to fear, not to be anxious, because of what the government authorities would charge.

Jesus was teaching them something that every Christian must learn. As Paul later reminded the Philippians, they were to be anxious for nothing (Philippians 4:6). Anxiety is a heart confessing that Christ is not Lord. To be worrisome is to think that we are ultimately in control, that we can alter our own circumstances, ultimately, by our own power.

The disciples were not to think this way. Jesus likely knew the kind of suffering that they would be called on to endure. He knew that the Christian road would be a rocky and bumpy one for them. He may have known that they would suffer martyrdom for their faith (see, for example, Matthew 20:23; Mark 10:39). To be worried about such things would have taken their mind off of the task at hand. It would have distracted them from the preaching of the gospel.

But in Luke's account, Jesus does not instruct his disciples not to be anxious, but "not to meditate beforehand." Why? Given Matthew's and Mark's account, what Jesus is saying is that they are not to set their minds on how they might respond when the challenges come from the governing authorities.

Matthew Henry's explanation of Luke 21:14 is worth remembering. He rightly understands Jesus to be saying something like this:

> Instead of setting your hearts on work to contrive an
> answer to informations, indictments, articles, accusa-
> tions, and interrogatories, that will be exhibited against
> you in the ecclesiastical and civil courts, on the contrary,
> settle it in your hearts, impress it upon them, take pains
> with them to persuade them not to meditate before what
> you shall answer; do not depend upon your own wit and
> ingenuity, your own prudence and policy, and do not
> distrust or despair of the immediate and extraordinary
> aids of the divine grace. Think not to bring yourselves
> off in the cause of Christ as you would in a cause of your
> own, by your own parts and application, with the com-
> mon assistance of divine Providence, but promise your-
> selves, for I promise you, the special assistance of divine
> grace: I will give you a mouth and wisdom.

It is this last statement that helps us see Christ's own focus in
this warning. If Jesus had told them not to meditate beforehand
on what they would say, it might be possible to read it as a universal prohibition—a warning against meditating beforehand
on anything and everything.

Third, in all three gospel accounts, the negative is followed
by a positive. Jesus tells his disciples not to worry, not to meditate beforehand, and then he tells them the positive. In Luke
the positive statement is, "For I will give you a mouth and wisdom, which none of your adversaries will be able to withstand
or contradict" (Luke 21:15). In Matthew (Mark is basically the
same) we read, "For what you are to say will be given to you in
that hour. For it is not you who speak, but the Spirit of your Father speaking through you" (10:19–20).

These positive statements help us to see what is meant in
the negative statements. In all three cases, Jesus emphasizes

what he, through the Holy Spirit, will give. This is where the Spirit's ministry, which we discussed above, is so crucial. The focus of Jesus' concern for his disciples is that they learn to rely on what the Holy Spirit gives them when they are challenged. And what is it that the Holy Spirit gives? According to Jesus, he will give them "all the truth" (John 16:13).

When they are challenged by the authorities, therefore, the disciples of Jesus Christ are to speak with mouths given by Christ, the wisdom that he alone gives at the time of challenge. What is required in situations like this is that the disciples know that truth, that they understand the wisdom that comes from above, that they use the very "speech" of God as given in his Word.

To put it into our context, Jesus' instruction, as a matter of fact, is the opposite of what it is sometimes thought to be. Rather than telling us not to prepare for the challenges to come, he is saying to us that we must be ready with the wisdom that is given from above. We must be ready, in other words, with the words of Scripture when our faith is challenged.

Our preparation, then, is not to focus on all the challenges that we might face, as if we could learn enough about all of them to answer them adequately. Rather, it is to focus on that which is given by God, "breathed out" by him, and therefore "profitable for teaching, for reproof, for correction, and for training in righteousness" (2 Timothy 3:16).

It is true, of course, that no one can be argued into the kingdom. But it is also true, in the Lord's wise plan, that no one will come to faith in Christ without hearing about that faith. As we defend the faith, and commend it to others, the Spirit promises to use us. What a privilege we have in Christ, to be agents of the Spirit himself as he glorifies the Son.

The Spirit breathes upon the Word,
And brings the truth to sight;
Precepts and promises afford
A sanctifying light.

A glory gilds the sacred page,
Majestic, like the sun:
It gives a light to every age;
It gives, but borrows none.

The Hand that gave it still supplies
The gracious light and heat:
His truths upon the nations rise;
They rise, but never set.

(William Cowper)

The Holy Spirit is, in the end, *the* apologist. As we meet the challenges that come, he glorifies Christ by taking his Word, as we speak, and convicting some of sin, righteousness, and judgment. He speaks in that Word, and, when he sees fit, he testifies to the hearts of some, who then turn and follow Christ—and join his battle!

SCRIPTURE PASSAGES
FOR APOLOGETICS

AS WE HAVE SEEN, the entire Bible can be seen as an apologetic. Having said that, however, there are a number of specific passages that can help us think through the principles discussed in this book. The list below is provided (1) as a supplement to the passages discussed in this book, and (2) as a beginning resource for a biblical study of apologetics.

This is by no means an exhaustive list of passages. There are many more that could be added. Because the focus of this book is on the New Testament, and because the New Testament is more familiar to most of us, this list focuses on Old Testament passages that have an apologetic thrust or theme to them. The list is provided for those who would like to study other biblical passages related to defending and commending the faith.

The Lord Our Defender

Exodus

14:13–31
15:1–18

Deuteronomy

7:9–11, 21–24
32:36–43
33:7, 27–29

Joshua

1:9
4:23–24
5:13–15
6:15–16
24:8–13

Judges

1:2, 22
4:13–16

1 Samuel

2:6–10
14:6

2 Samuel

22:2–20, 26–51

1 Kings

8:44–49

2 Kings

14:26–27
19:14–37
20:1–6

1 Chronicles

12:18
14:8–11
16:35
22:17–19
29:10–19

2 Chronicles

13:13–18
14:9–12
15:1–7
16:7–10
20:5–12, 22–23
25:7–8
32:20–23

Nehemiah

1
4:12–20
9:22–33

Job

2:4–6
9:1–12
12:13–25

Psalms

2
3:1–8
4
5
7:1–17
8:1–9
9:1–12, 19
10:1–18
11:4–7
12:3–8
14:4–7
16:1, 6–11
17
18:16–50
20:1–2
21:1–13
22:19–21
24:7–10
25:20–22
27:1–6
28:3–5
31:1–5, 13–24
33:10–22

34

35

36:7–12

37:12–29, 33, 39–40

38:21–22

40:1–3, 11–17

41:11–13

44:1–8

45:1–7

46:1–11

47

50:1–6

52:7–9

54

55:16–19, 22–23

56:1–13

57:1–6

58

59

61:1–4

62:1–2, 7

63:9–10

64

66:1–12

68:1–3, 17–21

69

70

71

73:18–20

74

75:4–8, 10

76

78:65–66

79

80:8–11

81:5–7

82

83

86:14–17

89:8–14, 50–51

90:17

91

92:9

94

97

99:1–4

102:12–22

103:13–14, 17–18

106:8–12

109:21–31

110

113:4–9

115:9–13

116

118:5–17

119:145–151

120

121:1–8

124:1–8

129:1–4

132:12–18

135:8–14

136:23–25

138:7–8

140

141:8–10

142

143

144

145:14, 17–21

146:5–10

147:1–6

149:4–9

Proverbs

11:8, 21

15:25

16:5, 11

18:10

21:1, 30–31

22:22–23

29:26

Isaiah

9:6–7

10:33–11:5

11:11–16

13:9–11

14:24–27, 32

22:1–5

24

28:5–6

33:20–22

34:1–7
35
37:15–20
40:1–5
41
42:1–4
49:22–26
50:7–9
52:6–12
56:1
63:8–14

Jeremiah

1:13–19
6:18–23
9:9–11
12:16–17
20:12–13
46
47
49:14–16
51:54–58

Lamentations

3:55–66

Ezekiel

25:12–17
26:19–21
28:1–10
32:1–16

35
36:33–38
38:19–23
39:1–24

Daniel

3:15–30
6:26–28
7:11–14

Amos

1:3–2:3

Obadiah

8–10

Jonah

2:1–9

Micah

5
7:7–10

Nahum

1:1–12

Habakkuk

3:19

Zephaniah

2

Haggai

2:1–9

Zechariah

9:14–17
10
12
13
14

Malachi

1:1–5
3:1–3
4:1–3

1 Corinthians

1:18–25
15:56–57

2 Corinthians

1:8–10
6:1–10

Ephesians

1:22–23

Colossians

2:13–15

2 Timothy

4:16–18

Revelation

1:7
6:1–2, 12–17
9:1–6

11:15–18
14:17–20
15
16

17:6–14
19:1–3, 11–21
20:1–5

OUR ATTITUDE IN DEFENSE

Genesis

22:16–19

Deuteronomy

28:1–14
32:44–47

Psalms

25:10–15, 21–22
39:1, 8
123:3–4
128:1–6
130:5–8

Proverbs

8:6–10
11:30–31
14:29
15:26
16:7, 18, 24

18:8
22:5
24:17–20
25:21–22
29:8
31:8–9

Acts

24:10–25
25:7–12

1 Corinthians

9:24–27
15:58
16:13–14

2 Corinthians

4:7–12
5:11, 20

Ephesians

6:10–20

1 Thessalonians

5:4–11

Titus

3:1–7, 9–10

Hebrews

12:14–15

James

4:1–10

1 Peter

3:8–17

Jude

3–4

WISDOM IN DEFENSE

Psalms

37:8, 30–31

15:1–5
111:10

119:25–29, 65–80,
130

Proverbs

2:1–15
3:7–8
4:7, 11–13
12:18–24
13:1, 10, 14, 20
14:3, 6, 15–16
15:6–7
16:21–23, 25
17:12
18:13, 15, 21
19:1–3, 8, 20–21, 25
21:16, 21–22, 29–30
22:10–12, 24–25
23:12
24:5–6, 10–11,
    15–16, 21–26,
    28–29
25:7–13
26:4–5, 12

28:7, 11, 26
29:9–11, 20
30:5–6

Jeremiah

8:8–9
9:12–16

Daniel

2:19–22

Hosea

14:9

Luke

21:10–19

Acts

19:8–9

1 Corinthians

10:12–13, 32–33

Colossians

2:1–4, 8–10
3:16–17
4:5–6

1 Thessalonians

2:3–4

2 Timothy

2:22–26

James

1:5–8
3

1 Peter

5:6–11

RELYING ON THE LORD

Deuteronomy

8:18

1 Chronicles

5:19–20

Psalms

4:4–5

5:7, 11–12
22:2–5
25:1–5
26:1–7
27
28:6–9
31:1–8, 17–18, 24
32:10–11

37:1–7, 34–38
39:7–9
40:4
55:23
60:10–12
62
69
78:21–22

80:1–3, 17–19

84:11–12

111:5–8

119:89–96

123:3–4

125:1–5

128

130:5–8

131

146:1–4

Proverbs

3:5–6

7:1–5, 24–27

11:28

14:26–27

16:20

19:23

20:22

21:2

22:4

23:17–18

28:25

29:25

Isaiah

12:2–4

25:8–9

26:1–8

31:1

40:28–31

43:10–12

50:10–11

Jeremiah

39:16–18

Acts

9:31

Romans

9:17

2 Corinthians

2:14–17

1 John

5:4–5

THE WICKED ENSNARED
BY THEIR OWN DEVICES

Psalms

9:15–16

10:2–3

69:22–23

73:3–12

81:15

92:6–8

Proverbs

5:22–23

6:12–15

8:35–36

10:10, 21, 24–25

12:10–14, 17, 26

13:9–10, 13, 21,
    25

14:1, 11–12, 18

18:1–3

19:5, 9

27:20, 22

28:5, 10, 14, 18

29:1, 6

Matthew

16:2–4

Philippians

3:18–19

INDEX OF SCRIPTURE CITED

K. Scott Oliphint (M.A.R., Th.M., Ph.D., Westminster Theological Seminary) is associate professor of apologetics at Westminster Seminary, Philadelphia. His ministry experience includes several years on the staff of Young Life and in the pastorate. He has written numerous articles on apologetics and is coauthor of *If I Should Die Before I Wake: Help for Those Who Hope for Heaven.*